CRANIUM CRACKERS
BOOK 2

SERIES TITLES:

CRANIUM CRACKERS BOOK 1
CRANIUM CRACKERS BOOK 2
CRANIUM CRACKERS BOOK 3
CRANIUM CRACKERS BOOK 4

Anita Harnadek

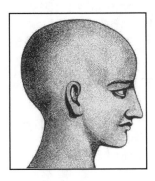

© 1997, 1991
THE CRITICAL THINKING CO.
(BRIGHT MINDS™)
www.CriticalThinking.com
P.O. Box 1610 • Seaside • CA 93955-1610
Phone 800-458-4849 • FAX 831-393-3277
ISBN 0-89455-665-7

TABLE OF CONTENTS

Add & Multiply
Other Bases 91-97

Add & Subtract
Clock Arithmetic 81-90

Addition
CrossNumber™ Puzzles 16-20
Replacing Letters 162

Analogies
Analogies in Proportions 104-122
Identifying Analogous Relationships 29-35
Rearranging Analogies 55-58
Reasoning by Analogy 36-39
Stating Analogies in Standard Form 53-54

Analogy Preparation
Finding Common Attributes 27
IdentifyingOopposites 21-23
Identifying the Outsider 28

Clock Arithmetic 81–90

Diophantine Problems 43, 98, 125, 152

Fractions
Analogies in Proportions 104-122
Index of Refraction 147
Miscellaneous Problems 163-164
Temperature Scales 135-137

Glossary 197

Index 198-199

Index of Refraction 147

Light-Years 144-146

Logic
Counterexamples 44-52
Drawing Inferences 4–15, 70-72
Fantasy or True to Life? 76-80
Math Mind Benders® 156-161
Mind Benders® 74-75, 140-143, 149
Miscellaneous Problems 1-2, 101-102
Water Jugs Problems 100, 124, 138, 154
Weighing Balls 103, 169

Mixed Operations
Miscellaneous Problems 126
Operators and Order of Precedence 59-69

Number Patterns 73, 165-166

Operators and Order of Precedence 59-69

Other Bases 91-97

Puzzles
CrossNumber™ Puzzles 16-20
Math Mind Benders® 156-161
Numbered Blanks 167
Rearrange Letters 40, 99, 123, 139, 153
Replacing Letters 162

Teaching Suggestions/Answers
Answers and Comments 172-196
Arithmetic Levels of This Series 171
General Information 170-171
Introduction 170
References 171-172
Teaching Thinking 172

Temperature Scales 135-137

Verbal Reasoning Problems
Drawing Inferences 4-15
Finding Common Attributes 27
Following Directions 3, 148
Identifying Analogous Relationships 29-35
Identifying Opposites 21-23
Identifying Synonyms 24-26
Identifying the Outsider 28
Rearranging Analogies 55-58
Reasoning by Analogy 36-39
Relevant Information 127-134
Stating Analogies in Standard Form 53-54

Word Problems
Diophantine Problems 43, 98 125, 152
Miscellaneous Problems 41-42, 101-102, 150-151, 155, 163-164, 168
Rearrange Letters 40, 99, 123, 139, 153

ACKNOWLEDGMENT

Mrs. Anderson, the principal of Elmwood Elementary School in South Lake School District, St. Clair Shores, Michigan, has my gratitude for her rundown of the kinds of arithmetic taught in Grades 3-4 and 5-6.

Reference

*Basic
Thinking
Skills*

MISCELLANEOUS PROBLEMS

PROBLEMS

1. Exactly twelve marbles are in a box. Six of the marbles are red, and the other six are green. The marbles are all mixed up so that they are not sorted by color.

    Someone blindfolds you and tells you to start picking marbles out of the box. He says you can't look to see what color you're choosing.

    What is the greatest number of marbles you'd have to take out of the box in order to make sure (still without seeing them) that you had two marbles of

    a. the same color? Tell why.

    b. different colors? Tell why.

    How does a plant seed know which way to grow? (How come it doesn't grow sideways or downwards when you drop it in the soil?)

Reference

*Basic
Thinking
Skills*

*Mind
Benders®
A1–A4*

2. A bulldog, a boxer, and a fox terrier each hid a bone. One bone was hidden under a hedge, one behind a tree, and one at the end of a short fence.

The next day the dogs couldn't remember where they hid their bones.

"I didn't hide mine by a hedge," said the bulldog.

"I know I didn't put mine near a tree," the fox terrier said.

"Neither did I," the bulldog remembered.

a. Which dog hid a bone under a hedge?

b. Which dog hid a bone behind a tree?

c. Which dog hid a bone at the end of a short fence?

Reference

Basic
Thinking
Skills

FOLLOWING DIRECTIONS

DIRECTIONS

Take a sheet of paper and a pencil (or pen). Each part of the problem tells you to do something. Do it all on the same sheet of paper.

PROBLEM

3. a. Draw a segment connecting the upper-right corner and the lower-left corner of your paper.

    b. Draw a segment connecting the upper-left corner and the lower-right corner of your paper.

    c. Put a dot about halfway between the upper-left corner and the center of your paper.

    d. Put a dot about halfway between the upper-right corner and the center of your paper.

    e. Draw a segment whose endpoints are the two dots you made.

    f. Write your name on the segment you drew for part e.

    g. Count the number of segments on your paper. Write this number just below your name. (Hint: There are more than ten.)

    h. Draw a square below the intersection of the segments you made in parts a and b.

    i. Multiply the number of days in a week by your answer for part g. Write the product inside the square.

DRAWING INFERENCES

DIRECTIONS

Sometimes a problem needs only a "yes" or "no" answer, but be ready to tell why you chose your answer if you are asked about it.

Sometimes a problem doesn't tell you enough to let you know for sure what the answer is. In this case, answer "not enough information."

PROBLEMS

4. Inez is shorter than Randall.

    Stephen is taller than Randall.

    List the names of the three people in the order of their height, starting with the tallest.

5. Jason's Aunt Georgina is married to his Uncle Robert.

    Jason has a cousin named Lucia.

    What is Lucia's relationship to Jason's Aunt Georgina and Uncle Robert?

6. There are three houses in a row.

One has aluminum siding.

Another has a red roof.

The third has a picture window.

You are standing in front of one of them.

The one with the aluminum siding is to your left.

The one with the picture window is to your right.

Where are you standing?

7. There are about 5 kilometers in 3 miles. Which is longer—a kilometer or a mile?

8. Jacob is older than Tasha and younger than Erica.

List the three names in the order of the people's ages, starting with the youngest.

Reference

Basic Thinking Skills

9. Read the three sentences below and then answer the question that follows.

    a. The teacher gave Ludwig's class a test today.

    b. Ludwig did not pass the test.

    c. Ludwig did not fail the test.

Can all three of those sentences be true? Explain.

10. You buy a package of hamburger buns for 70¢. You give the cashier a dollar bill to pay for it.

How much change should you get?

11. Sonia, Manuel, and Ismail all collect stamps.

Sonia has more stamps than Ismail.

Ismail has fewer stamps than Manuel.

List the three names in order, starting with the name of the person who has the least number of stamps.

Reference

Critical Thinking, Book 1

Inductive Thinking Skills

DIRECTIONS

You are given a short story. Tell whether each lettered sentence below the story is true (T), is false (F), or needs more information in order for you to decide (?).

• Accept the story as true. Try to forget anything you heard before about the story. Assume the story uses good English. In general, try to place yourself in the setting of the story.

• Use what you know unless the story says something different. For example, you know what a "house" is, but suppose the story says that only a blue tent can be a "house." Then you must believe the story, and you must not use your own idea of what a "house" is.

PROBLEMS

12. Story

THE PRINCESS AND THE FROG

While running one day, a beautiful princess fell into a well. She cried because she was unable to get out. A frog came along and said he would help her if she would do him a favor in return.

He said he was really a handsome prince who had been cast under a spell by a wicked sorcerer. He said the spell would be broken if a beautiful girl would kiss him. He said the princess was to kiss him in return for helping her get out of the well. The princess agreed to his terms.

a. The princess was beautiful.

b. The frog could talk.

c. The frog got the princess out of the well.

Reference

Critical Thinking, Book 1

Inductive Thinking Skills

d. The princess implied that she would kiss the frog if he got her out of the well.

e. The frog implied that he wouldn't help the princess if she wouldn't agree to kiss him.

f. The princess wept.

g. The frog was a handsome prince under a spell.

h. The frog liked being kissed by beautiful girls.

i. The princess must have been clumsy, since she fell into a well.

j. The sorcerer was wicked.

Reference

Critical Thinking, Book 1

Inductive Thinking Skills

13. Story

HANSEL AND GRETEL

Hansel and his older sister, Gretel, were lost in the woods. They walked and walked, and they finally saw a lovely house made of gingerbread.

Not knowing that the house belonged to the wicked witch, they knocked at the door. No one answered, and they went inside.

Being very hungry, they looked for something to eat. They opened the oven door to see if there was any food inside, whereupon the witch sneaked up behind them and pulled a large bag down over their heads and arms. The witch tied them up and dragged them over to a corner.

a. Hansel and Gretel were led into the woods by their father.

b. They had their bicycles with them.

c. They were looking for food when they opened the oven door.

d. Hansel was older than Gretel.

e. Hansel and Gretel were twins.

Reference

Critical Thinking, Book 1

Inductive Thinking Skills

f. The witch's cat told the witch that Hansel and Gretel were in the house.

g. The house wasn't made of gingerbread. The witch knew Hansel and Gretel were near, and she wanted to trap them, so she made the house *look* as though it were made of gingerbread, but it wasn't.

h. We need a definition of "woods" before we can decide whether or not Hansel and Gretel were lost.

i. No one answered the door when Hansel and Gretel knocked on it.

j. The birds in the trees tried to warn Hansel and Gretel that the house belonged to the witch.

Reference

Critical Thinking, Book 1

Inductive Thinking Skills

k. The witch was wicked.

l. Hansel and Gretel opened the oven door.

m. Hansel and Gretel weren't very hungry, but they were looking for food anyhow.

n. The witch was old.

o. The witch was beautiful.

p. Hansel and Gretel were related.

Reference

*Critical
Thinking,
Book 1*

*Inductive
Thinking
Skills*

q. Hansel and Gretel saw food in the oven.

r. The gingerbread house was in the woods.

s. The gingerbread house belonged to the witch.

t. Hansel and Gretel were children.

u. Hansel and Gretel knew that the house belonged to the witch.

v. Hansel and Gretel had a younger sister, Katina.

Reference

Critical Thinking, Book 1

Inductive Thinking Skills

14. Story

PETRA AND DIEGO AND SAM

Diego was five years younger than Petra and twice as old as Sam, their pet cat.

Sam liked to play with yarn and with her red ball.

a. Sam was the pet of both Diego and Petra.

b. Diego and Petra were brother and sister.

c. Diego and Petra were related.

d. Diego was five years old.

e. Sam was a dog.

Reference

Critical Thinking, Book 1

Inductive Thinking Skills

f. If Petra was nine years old, then Diego was four years old.

g. If Petra was nine years old, then Sam was one year old.

h. Sam was a female cat.

i. Diego was an adult.

j. Petra was seven years older than Sam.

k. Petra was at least seven years older than Sam.

Reference

Critical Thinking, Book 1

Inductive Thinking Skills

l. Sam could see in the dark.

m. Sam had stripes.

n. Petra was five years older than Diego.

o. Diego and Sam were closer in age than Petra and Sam were.

p. Diego and Sam were closer in age than Diego and Petra were.

q. Maybe the story lied when it said Sam was a cat.

Reference

*Cross-
Number™
Puzzles—
Sums,
Book A-1*

CrossNumber™ Puzzles

Lesson

A number *below* a diagonal shows a sum for the squares underneath. A number *above* a diagonal shows a sum for the squares to the right.

You are to write any digit from 1 through 9, one digit per square, so that their sums are correct. You may use a digit more than once in the puzzle, but you may not use it more than once for any one sum.

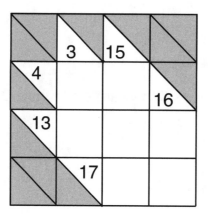

To solve the puzzle, look for sums that will be forced. (For example, don't start with 15 because there are several ways to get a sum of 15 from three digits.)

We will start with 3, which has to be either 1 + 2 or 2 + 1. See what happens when we try 2 + 1.

Now 4 has to be 2 + 2, but we are not allowed to use the same digit twice for a sum. So 3 has to be 1 + 2, and 4 is forced to be 1 + 3.

Reference

*Cross-
Number™
Puzzles—
Sums,
Book A-1*

The squares for 3 and 4 are filled in now, so we look for another sum to be forced. We choose 17, which must be either 8 + 9 or 9 + 8. If we use 9 + 8, the 8 will fall in one of 16's squares. But 16 can't be 8 + 8. So 17 has to be 8 + 9, and 16 is forced to be 7 + 9.

There is only one square left to be filled in, and that digit has to be the same for both 15 and 13.

We happened not to use any digit more than once in the puzzle, but the rules did not forbid it. The rules say only that we cannot use a digit more than once for any one sum.

Reference

Cross-Number™ Puzzles— Sums, Book A-1

DIRECTIONS

Fill in the grid so that the digits add up to the sums shown.

- A number below a diagonal shows the sum for the squares underneath.

- A number above a diagonal shows the sum for the squares to the right.

- You may use only the digits 1 through 9 (one digit per square).

- You may not use any digit more than once to get a sum.

PROBLEM

15.

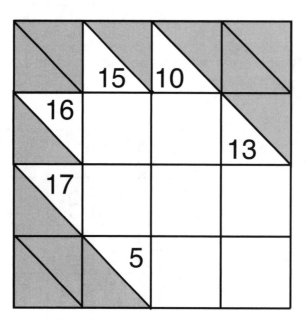

Reference

Cross-Number™ Puzzles— Sums, Book A-1

DIRECTIONS

Fill in the grid so that the digits add up to the sums shown.

- A number below a diagonal shows the sum for the squares underneath.

- A number above a diagonal shows the sum for the squares to the right.

- You may use only the digits 1 through 9 (one digit per square).

- You may not use any digit more than once to get a sum.

PROBLEM

16.

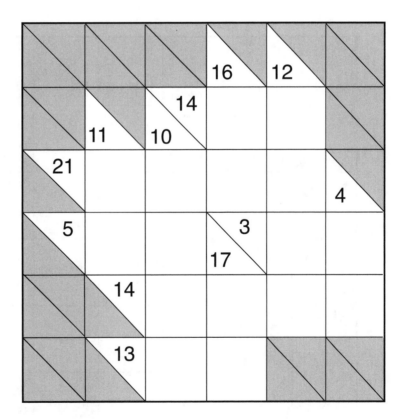

Reference

Cross-
Number™
Puzzles—
Sums,
Book B-1

DIRECTIONS

Fill in the grid so that the digits add up to the sums shown.

- A number below a diagonal shows the sum for the squares underneath.

- A number above a diagonal shows the sum for the squares to the right.

- You may use only the digits 1 through 9 (one digit per square).

- You may not use any digit more than once to get a sum.

PROBLEM

17.

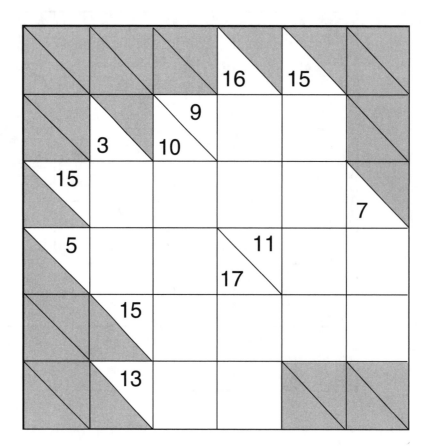

Reference

Basic Thinking Skills

IDENTIFYING OPPOSITES

DIRECTIONS

Each line contains several words.

Read the first word and think about what it means.

One of the other words will mean the *opposite* of the first word. Write this other word.

EXAMPLE

Problem: before (then, there, after)
Answer: after

PROBLEMS

18. ceiling (basement, ground, floor)

19. roof (basement, ground, floor)

20. early (prompt, late, punctual)

21. fact (disbelief, doubt, fiction)

22. fact (myth, rumor, gossip)

Reference

*Basic
Thinking
Skills*

23. speed (slow down, crawl, lag behind)

24. mansion (apartment, hovel, cottage)

25. spendthrift (lazybones, tightwad, conservative)

26. close (far, outside, ahead of, last)

27. close (unlock, open, reveal, start up)

28. kind (short-tempered, uppity, nasty, conceited)

Reference

*Basic
Thinking
Skills*

29.   right (left, up, down, backwards)

30.   right (doubtful, unsettled, questionable, wrong)

31.   dull (new, different, sharp, unused)

32.   dull (dangerous, engrossing, experimental, inventive)

33.   funny (boring, routine, usual, sad)

34.   boring (nonroutine, new, unusual, engrossing)

Reference

Basic Thinking Skills

IDENTIFYING SYNONYMS

DIRECTIONS

Each line contains several words.

Read the first word and think about what it means.

One of the other words will mean almost the same as the first word. Write this other word.

EXAMPLE

Problem: neat (messy, clean, tidy)

Answer: tidy

PROBLEMS

35. calm (peaceful, tired, asleep)

36. calm (warm, windy, windless)

37. net (nylon, mesh, flimsy material, thin material)

38. net (hunt, track, catch, chase)

39. net (profit, total, gift, score)

Reference

*Basic
Thinking
Skills*

40.   foul (track, rotten, illegal, bird)

41.   fowl (track, rotten, illegal, bird)

42.   pare (peel, cover, kind of fruit, set of two)

43.   pare (reduce, kind of fruit, set of two, increase)

44.   pear (peel, kind of fruit, set of two, reduce)

45.   pair (peel, kind of fruit, set of two, reduce)

Reference

*Basic
Thinking
Skills*

46.   seen (vista, sighted, sensed, noticed)

47.   scene (vista, sighted, sensed, noticed)

48.   cent (odor, penny, dispatched, judgment)

49.   sent (odor, penny, dispatched, judgment)

50.   scent (odor, penny, dispatched, judgment)

51.   sense (odor, penny, dispatch, judgment)

Reference

Basic Thinking Skills

FINDING COMMON ATTRIBUTES

DIRECTIONS

Each line contains four words. Read all four words.

The four words will all have something in common. Decide what this common thing is, and write it down.

EXAMPLE

Problem: ball, wheel, plate, coin
Answer: round shape

PROBLEMS

52. finished, concluded, over, through

53. before, earlier, preceding, prior to

54. double, twin, clone, duplicate

55. liter, pint, quart, gallon

56. castle, manor, mansion, palace

57. beret, tam, beanie, cap

Reference

*Basic
Thinking
Skills*

IDENTIFYING THE OUTSIDER

DIRECTIONS

Read the five given terms. Four of the terms have something in common. The other term does not have this same quality.

Tell what the four terms have in common, and tell which term doesn't belong.

EXAMPLE

Problem: nice, big, mean, kind, nasty

Answer: ways to describe personality; big

PROBLEMS

58. accidental, designed, intentional, on purpose, planned

59. fresh, just picked, unwilted, newly baked, well-preserved

60. fresh, sassy, cheeky, insulting, pert

61. fresh, cautious, vigilant, alert, wide-awake

62. fresh, new, modern, popular, current

63. mansion, palace, castle, manor, cottage

Reference

*Basic
Thinking
Skills*

IDENTIFYING ANALOGOUS RELATIONSHIPS

DIRECTIONS

Each problem takes up two lines. There are two terms on the first line. There are at least four terms on the second line.

On the first line, read the two terms and figure out how they are related. Then go to the second line and find this same relationship between the first term there and one of the other terms there.

Write the word you choose.

EXAMPLE

Problem: kind, unkind

nice, (big, hungry, nasty)

Answer: nasty

PROBLEMS

64. long, length
wide, (height, area, width)

65. go in, go out
enter, (door, exit, elevator)

66. guffaw, giggle
bawl, (whimper, weep, brown)

Reference

*Basic
Thinking
Skills*

67. inactive, active
lazy, (powerful, wakeful, lively, headstrong)

68. teacher, student
teach, (hear, listen, learn, obey)

69. 12 ÷ 3, 4
12 ÷ 2, (2, 3, 4, 6)

70. touch, feel
eat, (drink, food, meal, taste)

71. lawyer, attorney
doctor, (bookkeeper, nurse, physician, secretary)

Reference

Basic Thinking Skills

DIRECTIONS

Each problem takes two or three lines.

There are two terms on the first line. Read these terms and figure out how they are related.

On the other lines are some *pairs* of terms. Choose the pair whose words are related in the same way as the terms on the first line.

EXAMPLE

Problem: hard, soft
       (work, play / cement, mud / mud, steel)
Answer: cement, mud

PROBLEMS

72. plus, minus
(less, more / quotient, product / sum, difference)

73. less, minus
(add, subtract / divide, add / more, plus / subtract, difference)

74. true, false
(fact, fiction / current news, history / elephant, dinosaur)

Reference

*Basic
Thinking
Skills*

75. male, female
(gentleman, lady / carpenter, secretary / fire fighter, homemaker)

76. year, 12 months
(hour, 60 seconds / month, 4 weeks / sun, moon / week, 7 days)

77. right, wrong
(laugh, cry / tidy, messy / clear, foggy / good, evil)

78. right, wrong
(exact, approximate / knowledge, guess / correct, incorrect / direct, indirect)

79. donate, accept
(give, take / lesson, homework / buy, sell / promise, believe)

DIRECTIONS

Each problem is given in the form of a chart.

The words for the last two columns are listed (by column, in alphabetical order) below the chart.

Each line of the chart is a small problem by itself.

For each line, read the first two words and decide how they are related. Then find a third and fourth word (from the bottom) that are related in the same way.

EXAMPLE

Problem:

able	unable		
active	inactive		
ask	why		
fleas	dog		
quarter	1/4		

Column 3: alive, answer, can, half, lice
Column 4: because, cannot, dead, human, 1/2

Answer:

able	unable	can	cannot
active	inactive	alive	dead
ask	why	answer	because
fleas	dog	lice	human
quarter	1/4	half	1/2

PROBLEMS

80.

fry	egg		
may	must		
old	young		
yesterday	today		
strong	weak		

Column 3: aged, bake, before, permit, sturdy
Column 4: cake, frail, now, order, youthful

Reference

*Basic
Thinking
Skills*

81.

add	multiply		
add	subtract		
add	sum		
add	enlarge		
add	increase		

Column 3: deduct, plus, plus, subtract, subtract
Column 4: decrease, difference, minus, reduce, times

REASONING BY ANALOGY

LESSON

When you reason by *analogy* (uh NAL uh jee), you think, "This situation is a lot like that other situation. Therefore, the same thing will be true now that was true then."

In other words, an analogy looks at two things and says, "They are alike in some ways. So they are also alike in these other ways."

Some analogies are good ones, and some are not.

EXAMPLE 1

When Ezra takes a test, he closes his eyes while he thinks of an answer. He finishes at least fifteen minutes early, and he always gets good test grades. I want to get good test grades, so I'm going to close my eyes while I think of an answer, and I'm going to finish at least fifteen minutes early.

The two things being compared are (1) what Ezra does when he takes a test and (2) what I will do when I take the same test. I notice two things that Ezra does and that I intend to do, so the situations are alike in at least two ways. I figure that they should also be alike in the test grades Ezra and I get.

This is a very poor analogy. Ezra's test grades depend on the answers he gives, not on whether or not he closes his eyes or finishes early. So the two situations are not enough alike to make my conclusion reasonable.

EXAMPLE 2

Ezra studies before a test and he always gets good test grades. I asked him how he knows what to study, and he told me. I'm as smart as Ezra is, so if I study before a test like Ezra does, I should get good test grades, too.

This is a good analogy. In a case like this, the situations are said to be analogous.

Reference

*Inductive
Thinking
Skills*

DIRECTIONS

You are told about an analogy someone has used.

Tell whether you think the analogy is pretty good, just okay, poor, or needs more information in order for you to decide.

Whatever you answer, tell why.

PROBLEM

82. Henry's arithmetic class has been studying fractions for a month now. Henry understood arithmetic easily up until then, but he finds fractions hard to understand.

The same thing happened three years ago to his sister Bethany, who is smarter than Henry, and she has had trouble learning arithmetic ever since.

Henry concludes that he, too, will have trouble understanding arithmetic from now on.

Reference

Inductive Thinking Skills

DIRECTIONS

You are told about an analogy someone has used.

Tell whether you think the analogy is pretty good, just okay, poor, or needs more information in order for you to decide.

Whatever you answer, tell why.

PROBLEM

83. When Janine went to Lila's house and petted Lila's yellow cat, Janine started sneezing and kept sneezing until Lila got her a glass of water and the cat walked away. This happened every time Janine petted the cat.

Today, Janine is at the house of Doris, a new classmate. Doris, too, has a yellow cat. Janine refuses to pet it because she knows she always sneezes when she pets a yellow cat.

Reference

Inductive Thinking Skills

DIRECTIONS

You are told about an analogy someone has used.

Tell whether you think the analogy is pretty good, just okay, poor, or needs more information in order for you to decide.

Whatever you answer, tell why.

PROBLEM

84. Yesterday Antonio hit his first home run, and the baseball bat cracked.

He knows that baseball bats don't crack every time a home run is hit, but the bat really connected solidly with the ball for his home run.

He concluded that the next time he hits a baseball the same way he did for his home run yesterday, that bat will crack, too.

REARRANGE LETTERS

DIRECTIONS

Use the letters at the top to fill in the chart so that words are formed and the sentence makes sense.

- A shaded space in the chart shows the end of a word. Two shaded spaces together show the end of a sentence.

- Except for the last line, the end of a line is not the end of a word unless there is a shaded space there.

- When you have filled in the chart, answer the question asked.

PROBLEM

85.

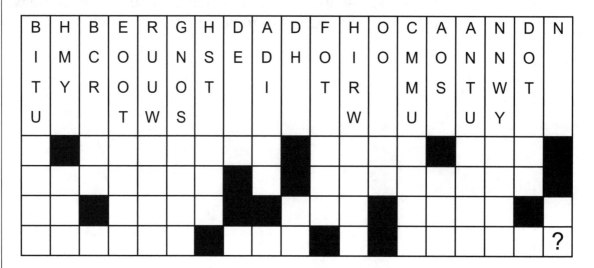

Reference

Classroom Quickies— Book 3

MISCELLANEOUS PROBLEMS

PROBLEMS

86. You're out walking in the country one day and you see this gorgeous pig. It's green with purple stripes and pink polka dots, and it has long eyelashes and a nice smile and it's the most beautiful thing you've ever seen.

So you go home and scrape together all the money you've saved from doing odd jobs in the past three years, and you go back and buy the pig for $40.

You take the pig home and your parents say you can't keep it, so you sell it for $50. Then your parents change their mind, and you buy it back for $60.

Then your landlord finds out about the pig and says you'll have to get rid of it, so you sell it again for $70.

OK, so you bought it for $40, sold it for $50, bought it back again for $60, and sold it again for $70. All together, how much did you gain or lose on these combined deals?

Reference

Classroom Quickies— Books 2 & 3

87. A woodsman is taking a fox, a goose, and some corn to town. He has to cross a stream and must cross a slippery log in order to get to the other side, so he decides to take the three things over one at a time.

If he leaves the fox with the goose, the fox will eat the goose. If he leaves the goose with the corn, the goose will eat the corn.

How does he get the three things safely across the stream?

What do you call a muddy chicken who crosses a road twice?

Reference

Algebra
Word
Problems—
Diophan-
tine
Problems

Classroom
Quickies—
Books 1–3

Diophantine Problems

Problem

88. Jonathan is rotten at playing marbles and almost always loses to his sister Eunice, who never gives back the marbles Jonathan loses to her.

Jonathan heard about a sale of marbles where shooters are 5¢ each, red marbles are 3¢ each, and multicolored marbles are 5 for a penny.

He has a dollar to spend and has decided to buy 100 marbles so that he won't run out for a while.

How many of each kind of marble can he buy?

(Hint: There is more than one answer to this problem.)

Why does a forest ranger wear green suspenders?

Reference

Critical Thinking— Books 1 & 2

COUNTEREXAMPLES

LESSON

Some statements are false but cannot be proved false. For example, suppose I told you that I've always wanted a zebra. I haven't, but there is no way for you to prove that I lied to you.

Other statements are false and can be proved false. For instance, suppose I said that everyone wants a zebra. My words will be proved false if you find one person who does *not* want a zebra. That one person will be a *counterexample* to my statement.

A counterexample to a statement is a specific example that proves the statement is false.

EXAMPLE

Statement: Every dog is green.

These are counterexamples:

My dog is pink.

My sister's dog isn't green.

Mrs. MacDonald's dog is orange with black spots.

These are not counterexamples:

I don't believe that. (No example is given.)

No dog is green. (No example is given.)

My cat is black. (This doesn't make the statement false.)

No bulldog is green. (This proves the statement false, but it is not a counterexample because it is not a *specific* example.)

Only certain kinds of statements can have counterexamples to them. (The next lesson will say more about this.) For these kinds of statements, counterexamples are nearly always the easiest way to prove the statements are not true.

Reference

Critical Thinking— Books 1 & 2

DIRECTIONS

A statement is given and is followed by several lettered sentences.

Tell whether or not each lettered sentence is a counterexample to the statement, and tell why.

PROBLEM

89. Statement: All dogs are purple.

    a. My dog is white.

    b. Parrots are purple, too.

    c. I've seen lots of dogs, but never a purple one.

    d. No dog in my neighborhood is purple.

    e. My uncle has a purple dog.

    f. My neighbor's dog isn't purple.

    g. There must be a dog that isn't purple somewhere in the world.

Reference

Critical Thinking— Books 1 & 2

LESSON CONT.

A counterexample contradicts a statement about everything of a kind. This means that only certain kinds of statements can have counterexamples.

These statements are about everything of a kind. There may be counterexamples to these statements.

All dogs are green.

No dog is green.

If something is a dog, then it is green.

No single example will prove any of these next statements false because the statements are not about everything of a kind. Such statements can have no counterexamples.

Some dogs are green.

Many dogs are green.

Only a few dogs are green.

Notice that a counterexample to a statement proves that the statement is false in one case, but it doesn't prove that the statement is false in every case. In other words, a counterexample simply shows that the statement should not have been made about *everything*.

EXAMPLE

Statement: All dogs are green.

Counterexample: My dog isn't green.

The counterexample proves the statement false, but it doesn't prove that no dog is green.

Reference

Critical Thinking— Books 1 & 2

DIRECTIONS

Tell whether or not each lettered statement is the kind of statement for which a counterexample might be found.

In other words, tell whether or not the statement could be proved false by finding just one example.

PROBLEM

90. a. Everybody should learn how to use a dictionary.

b. Most computer games are fun to play.

c. Nobody enjoys being yelled at.

d. All Little League baseball games are fun.

e. Some people are very hard to please.

f. Adults are almost never as polite to children as they are to other adults.

g. If you haven't been doing well in school, it's because you haven't been studying.

DIRECTIONS

A statement is given and is followed by lettered sentences.

Tell whether or not each lettered sentence is a counterexample to the statement. If it is not, then tell why not.

EXAMPLE

Problem: All boys like to play baseball.

    a. Brett is a boy, and he doesn't like to play baseball.

    b. Cathy is a girl, and she likes to play baseball.

Answers: a. Yes

    b. No. The statement does not say anything about what girls like or don't like.

PROBLEMS

91. If kids wouldn't fool around so much in school, then they'd learn more.

    a. That's what my mother said, so I stopped fooling around in school, and I'm not learning any more now than I did before.

    b. Kids fool around in school only once in a while, and that isn't enough to keep them from learning.

    c. Bill always learns everything that is taught, and he fools around all the time.

Reference

Critical Thinking— Books 1 & 2

92. Almost everyone has a sense of humor.

    a. My kindergarten teacher had no sense of humor at all.

    b. That's because people like to laugh.

    c. They don't think it's funny when the joke is on them.

93. All children like to play games.

    a. My little cousin broke her leg, and so she can't play games for a while.

    b. My next-door neighbor is a ten-year-old genius, and he never plays games.

    c. My aunt likes to play games, and she isn't a child.

    d. My brother doesn't like to play games, and he's eight years old.

Reference

Critical Thinking— Books 1 & 2

94. Very few people would rather read a book than watch TV.

　a. My uncle always seems to be reading a book.

　b. I think TV is boring, and I'd rather read an adventure book.

　c. Mary Ann would rather watch a movie on TV than read the book the movie came from.

95. Nobody likes to play baseball in the rain.

　a. That isn't even an intelligent thing to say because they call off a baseball game when it rains.

　b. I like to play baseball any time.

　c. Football is played in the rain, so I don't see why baseball shouldn't be, too.

　d. My uncle doesn't mind playing baseball with me whether it's raining or not.

Reference

Critical Thinking— Books 1 & 2

96. Suppose a statement about everything of a kind is true. Can there be a counterexample to it? If so, give an example. If not, how come?

97. Suppose you are given the statement,

"All zoffers are middigs,"

and you find a zoffer that is not a middig. Have you

a. found a counterexample to the statement?

b. proved the statement false?

c. proved that no zoffers are middigs?

d. proved that at least one zoffer is not a middig?

e. proved that if anything is a zoffer, then it is not a middig?

f. proved that if anything is a zoffer, then it is not necessarily a middig?

g. proved that if anything is not a zoffer, then it is a middig?

h. proved that if anything is a middig, then it is not a zoffer?

i. proved that some (at least one) middigs are not zoffers?

Reference

Critical Thinking— Books 1 & 2

98. Suppose you are given the statement,

"All zoffers are middigs,"

and you find a middig that is not a zoffer. Have you

a. found a counterexample to the statement?

b. proved the statement false?

c. proved that no zoffers are middigs?

d. proved that at least one zoffer is not a middig?

e. proved that if anything is a zoffer, then it is not a middig?

f. proved that if anything is a zoffer, then it is not necessarily a middig?

g. proved that if anything is not a zoffer, then it is a middig?

h. proved that if anything is not a zoffer, then it is not a middig?

i. proved that if anything is a middig, then it is not a zoffer?

j. proved that some (at least one) middigs are not zoffers?

STATING ANALOGIES IN STANDARD FORM

LESSON

Suppose we find a relation between two things, and we find the same relation between two other things.

Then we say there is an *analogous* (uh NAL uh gus) relationship between the two pairs.

EXAMPLE

There is an analogous relationship between the pair

> hot   cold

and the pair

> steam   ice.

To state the analogy (uh NAL uh jee) between the two pairs, we will use the words "is to" and "as":

> *Hot* is to *cold* as *steam* is to *ice.*

DIRECTIONS

Each problem takes two or three lines. On the first line are a pair of terms. Figure out how they are related. On the other lines are several pairs of terms. Choose the pair that are analogous to the pair on the first line. Then state the analogy between the two pairs.

EXAMPLE

Problem: hot, cold

> (big, little / ice, steam / steam, ice / right, wrong)

Answer: Hot is to cold as steam is to ice.

PROBLEMS

99. man, woman

> (beard, wig / male, female / lawyer, secretary)

100. mayor, city

(country, county / corporation, president / governor, state)

101. fact, fiction

(rumor, gossip / history, myth / newspaper, book)

102. snow, ski

(water, swim / plane, pilot / school, student)

103. master, slave

(man, woman / university, high school / ruler, subject)

104. hammer, saw

(cut, pound / hit, cut / plumber, carpenter / metal, wood)

REARRANGING ANALOGIES

LESSON

If we find an analogy between two pairs of things, we can rearrange the four things so that there are other analogies, too.

For instance, with the two pairs

hot, cold / steam, ice

all of these would be correct:

Hot	is to	cold	as	steam	is to	ice.
Cold	is to	hot	as	ice	is to	steam.
Steam	is to	ice	as	hot	is to	cold.
Ice	is to	steam	as	cold	is to	hot.
Hot	is to	steam	as	cold	is to	ice.
Steam	is to	hot	as	ice	is to	cold.
Cold	is to	ice	as	hot	is to	steam.
Ice	is to	cold	as	steam	is to	hot.

Don't be fooled into thinking an analogy will be correct no matter how you position the terms.

There are 24 ways to list 4 terms, and only 8 of these will work.

Here are some of the 16 incorrect arrangements for the four terms above:

Hot	is to	cold	as	ice	is to	steam.
Hot	is to	ice	as	cold	is to	steam.
Steam	is to	ice	as	cold	is to	hot.
Cold	is to	ice	as	steam	is to	hot.

DIRECTIONS

You are given four terms. If they can be split into analogous pairs, list at least three correct analogies.

EXAMPLE

Problem: speaker, hear, talk, listener

Answer: (Any three of these would be correct.)

Speaker is to talk as listener is to hear.

Speaker is to listener as talk is to hear.

Hear is to listener as talk is to speaker.

Hear is to talk as listener is to speaker.

Talk is to speaker as hear is to listener.

Talk is to hear as speaker is to listener.

Listener is to speaker as hear is to talk.

Listener is to hear as speaker is to talk.

PROBLEMS

105. pencil, ink, pen, lead

106. grass, garden, lawn, flower

107. fan, heater, cool, warm

108. eyes, hear, ears, feel

109. sight, sound, ears, eyes

DIRECTIONS

This problem is just for fun.

Each one of the four entries is a term for an analogy. The terms are arranged in the right order for an analogy, but they may be disguised by puns, misspellings, homonyms, misleading definitions, and other good things.

Figure out what the correct terms are, and write the analogy.

PROBLEM

110.

1/3 of a fenced lawn

paper and pencil game for two with no clock sound or sharp object

penmanship without writing

fish structure followed by sound of cross dog

DIRECTIONS

This problem is just for fun.

Each one of the four entries is a term for an analogy. The terms are arranged in the right order for an analogy, but they may be disguised by puns, misspellings, homonyms, misleading definitions, and other good things.

Figure out what the correct terms are, and write the analogy.

PROBLEM

111.

roller coaster with no hair curler

window pane

place tahhsittocS

LP without tr

OPERATORS AND ORDER OF PRECEDENCE

LESSON

Addition (+), subtraction (−), multiplication (×), and division (÷ or /) are arithmetic *operators*.

A problem can include an operator more than once:

$$5 + 3 + 4 = ?$$

It can also include different operators:

$$6 + 10 − 4 = ?$$

$$15 ÷ 3 + 2 = ?$$

Parentheses can be used to show which operator to start with:

$$(15 ÷ 3) + 2 = ?$$

$$15 ÷ (3 + 2) = ?$$

To solve a problem, we move from left to right, but we must do it in this order:

1. ( )

2. ×, ÷ or / (These operators have equal importance. Start at the left and do whichever one comes first. Keep going and do whichever one comes next.)

3. +, − (These operators have equal importance.)

For the examples below, remember the rules: move from left to right, but first do ( ), then do × and ÷ and /, and then do + and −.

EXAMPLE 1

Problem: $1 + 2 \times 3$

Solution:

Step 1. There are no ( ), so skip this step.

Step 2. Do ×, ÷, and /. There is no ÷ or /, so do 2×3 and get $1 + 2 \times 3 = 1 + 6$.

Step 3. Do + and −. There is no −, so $1 + 6 = 7$.

Answer: $1 + 2 \times 3 = 1 + 6 = 7$

EXAMPLE 2

Problem: $(1 + 2) \times 3$

Solution:

Step 1. Do ( ). So $(1 + 2) \times 3 = 3 \times 3$.

Step 2. Do ×, ÷, and /. So $3 \times 3 = 9$. We are through now, so we don't need step 3.

Answer: $(1 + 2) \times 3 = 3 \times 3 = 9$

EXAMPLE 3

Problem: $5 + 12/(1 + 3)$

Solution:

Step 1. Do ( ). We get $5 + 12/(1 + 3) = 5 + 12/4$.

Step 2. Do ×, ÷, and /. We get $5 + 12/4 = 5 + 3$.

Step 3. Do + and −. We get $5 + 3 = 8$.

Answer: $5 + 12/(1 + 3) = 5 + 12/4 = 5 + 3 = 8$

EXAMPLE 4

Problem: 14 – (6 ÷ 3 + 5)

Solution:

Step 1. Do ( ). So do 6 ÷ 3 + 5. This is like example 1. The answer is 6 ÷ 3 + 5 = 2 + 5 = 7. We can now write the example 4 problem like this: 14 – (6 ÷ 3 + 5) = 14 – 7.

Step 2. There is no ÷ now, so skip this step.

Step 3. Do –. We get 14 – 7 = 7.

Answer: 14 – (6 ÷ 3 + 5) = 14 – (2 + 5) = 14 – 7 = 7

EXAMPLE 5

Problem: (3 + 12 ÷ 3) × (6 – 4 + 2)

Solution:

Step 1. Do ( ). There are two sets of ( ). The rule is, work from left to right. So 3 + 12 ÷ 3 will be done first, and then 6 – 4 + 2 will be done. For 3 + 12 ÷ 3, we remember to do ÷ before +, and we get 3 + 12 ÷ 3 = 3 + 4 = 7. For 6 – 4 + 2, the + and – have equal rank, so we go left to right and get 6 – 4 + 2 = 2 + 2 = 4. We now have (3 + 12 ÷ 3) × (6 – 4 + 2) = 7 × 4.

Step 2. Do ×. We get 7 × 4 = 28. We don't need step 3.

Answer: (3 + 12 ÷ 3) × (6 – 4 + 2) =
(3 + 4) × (6 – 4 + 2) =
7 × (6 – 4 + 2) =
7 × (2 + 2) = 7 × 4 = 28

EXAMPLE 6

Problem: 20 ÷ 10/2 × 7

Solution: We don't need step 1 or step 3 for this one. Step 2 says the operators ×, ÷, and / are all of equal rank and we are to work from left to right.

Answer: 20 ÷ 10/2 × 7 = 2/2 × 7 = 1 × 7 = 7

Notice that the answer would be different if ( ) enclosed 10/2. Then we would have 20 ÷ (10/2) × 7 = 20 ÷ 5 × 7 = 4 × 7 = 28.

DIRECTIONS

You are told what answer is wanted.

To get this answer, you may use only the numbers 2, 3, and 6, along with two operators. You may *not* use ( ).

Show your work in the same way the example below shows the work.

EXAMPLE

Problem: Get an answer of 4.

Answer: $6 \times 2 \div 3 = 12 \div 3 = 4$

For each answer, you must use each of the numbers 2, 3, and 6 exactly once.

You may use the same operator twice if you wish to do so.

You are not allowed to combine digits to make a new number. For example, you are not allowed to combine 2 and 6 and get 26.

There are different ways to get each answer, so do not copy the example's arrangement for your answer.

PROBLEMS

112. Get an answer of 0.

113. Get an answer of 1.

114. Get an answer of 4.

115. Get an answer of 5.

116. Get an answer of 6.

117. Get an answer of 7.

118. Get an answer of 9.

119. Get an answer of 11.

120. Get an answer of 12.

> **DIRECTIONS**
>
> Find the answer for each problem. Show your work.

PROBLEMS

121. $4 \times 3 \div 2$

122. $7 - 2 \times 3$

123. $1 + 8 - 3 \times 2$

124. $1 + (8 - 3) \times 2$

125. $(1 + 8 - 3) \div 2$

126. $(8 - 3 \times 2) + 11$

127. $4 \times 6/(3 + 25 \div 5)$

128. $2 \times (24 - 3 \times 3 + 7 - 2 \times 9)$

129. $14 - (2 \times 8 + 2) \div (63 \div 7)$

130. $57 - (3 \times 7 - 15) \times (5 + 12 \div 4)$

131. $72 \div (14 - 24 \div 4) \times (16 - 11) - 4 \times 5$

DIRECTIONS

Insert ( ) so that the problem's answer will be the answer given.

If no ( ) are needed, then don't insert any.

Show your work as the examples do.

EXAMPLE 1

Problem: $1 + 4 \times 3$; answer 15

Answer: $(1 + 4) \times 3 = 5 \times 3 = 15$

EXAMPLE 2

Problem: $1 + 4 \times 3$; answer 13

Answer: $1 + 4 \times 3 = 1 + 12 = 13$

PROBLEMS

132. $2 + 4/2$; answer 3

133. $18 - 6 + 12/3$; answer 8

134. $13 + 5/2 \times 7$; answer 63

135. $2 \times 6 - 1 + 8$; answer 3

136. $7 \times 8 - 5 \times 10$; answer 6

137. $24/6/2 + 3$; answer 11

138. $14 \div 1 + 6 \times 8 - 1$; answer 15

139. $48 \div 12 - 4 \times 14 - 5$; answer 54

140. $4 + 2 \times 7 - 9 \times 4$; answer 6

141. $2 + 3 \times 6 - 3 \times 7 + 1$; answer 8

142. $4 \times 12/2 + 1 + 2 - 5 \times 6$; answer 0

Reference

Classroom Quickies— Books 1–3

143. Using the digits 1, 2, 3, and 4, along with any mathematical operators you choose, see how many different numbers you can write.

Here are the rules:

Your answers must be whole numbers.

In each answer, you must use each of the four digits exactly once.

You are allowed to use any mathematical symbols and operators you know about. For example, you may use decimals and ( ) if you understand them.

In each answer, you may use any operator as often as you like.

You are allowed to use each digit as a separate number.

You are allowed to combine two or more digits to make a number.

If you combine two digits to make a number, you cannot use an operator to separate the digits. For example, you may use 1 and 2 to make the number 21, but you may not write something like

$$2(4 - 3)$$

to make 21. If you understand decimals, you are allowed to use a decimal point between two digits. For example, you could write

$$1.2$$

to make one and two tenths.

EXAMPLES

$$0 = 1 + 4 - 2 - 3$$

$$1 = 2 \times 3 - 4 - 1$$

$$2 = (2 + 4) \div 3 \times 1$$

$$3 = (4 + 2) \times 1 - 3$$

$$4 = 2 \times 4 - 1 - 3$$

$$5 = 2 \times 4 \times 1 - 3$$

$$6 = 12/4 + 3$$

Reference

Classroom Quickies— Books 1–3

144. This problem is like the preceding one, except that this time you are to use only 4s, along with any mathematical operators you choose.

For each problem, you must use at least two 4s, and you may not use more than six 4s.

See how many different numbers you can write.

Here are the rules again:

Your answers must be whole numbers.

You are allowed to use any mathematical symbols and operators you know about. For example, you may use decimals and ( ) if you understand them.

In each answer, you may use any operator as often as you like.

You are allowed to use each 4 as a separate number.

You are allowed to combine two or more 4s to make a number.

If you combine two or more 4s to make a number, you cannot use an operator to separate the digits. For example, you may use two 4s to make the number 44, but you may not write something like

$$4(4 + 4 - 4)$$

to make 44. If you understand decimals, you are allowed to use a decimal point between two digits. For example, you could write

$$4.4$$

to make four and four tenths.

EXAMPLES

$$0 = 4 - 4$$
$$1 = 4 \div 4$$
$$2 = (4 + 4)/4$$
$$3 = 4 - 4/4$$
$$4 = 4 \times 4/4$$
$$5 = 4 + 4/4$$
$$6 = 4 + (4 + 4)/4$$

Reference

Basic
Thinking
Skills

DRAWING INFERENCES

DIRECTIONS

Sometimes a problem needs only a "yes" or "no" answer, but be ready to tell why you chose your answer if you are asked about it.

Sometimes a problem doesn't tell you enough to let you know for sure what the answer is. In this case, answer "not enough information."

PROBLEMS

145. Lucretia caught a bus at 7:10 a.m. and rode it for 5 miles. Jennifer caught a bus at the opposite end of town at 7:18 a.m. and rode it for 5 miles. Both left their buses at the same time. How can that be explained?

146. There are 1,760 yards in a mile. Which is longer—a mile, or 2,000 yards?

147. Betty is shorter than Arthur but older than he is. Mortimer is taller than Arthur but younger than he is. Starting with the least, list the three names in the order of the
a. heights

b. ages

Reference

*Basic
Thinking
Skills*

148. Two men, Mark and Lawrence, are not related to each other. Joan and Helen are their sisters. Mark is the manager of a supermarket. Lawrence is an attorney. Joan is a judge. Helen is a wood-carver.

Who is Mark's sister? Who is Lawrence's sister?

149. Go back to problem 148. Suppose you are also told that a brother and sister do not work in related fields.

Now who is Mark's sister? Who is Lawrence's sister?

150. An ice-cube tray holds sixteen ice cubes. How many ice cubes will two ice-cube trays hold?

Reference

*Basic
Thinking
Skills*

151. Lester weighs more than Abraham.

Abraham weighs more than Bradley.

Does Lester weigh more than Bradley?

152. Graham is the father of Edmund.

Edmund is the father of Frederick.

Is Graham the father of Frederick?

153. Catherine is the cousin of Francine.

Francine is the cousin of Yvette.

Is Catherine the cousin of Yvette?

Reference

*Basic
Thinking
Skills*

NUMBER PATTERNS

DIRECTIONS

Copy each problem.

Each problem lists some numbers and some blanks. Find a pattern formed by the numbers listed.

Fill in the blanks so that the pattern is continued. (You may find more than one pattern. If so, use any pattern you find.)

EXAMPLE

Problem: 1, 2, 3, 4, __, __, __, __

One answer: 1, 2, 3, 4, _5_, _6_, _7_, _8_ (Here, the pattern is a simple counting pattern.)

Another answer: 1, 2, 3, 4, _7_, _8_, _15_, _16_ (Here, the pattern is as follows: Add the first two numbers to get the next number; add 1 to get the number after that; add the two new numbers to get the third new number; add 1 to get the next number; continue in the same way.)

PROBLEMS

154. 1, 3, 4, 6, 7, __, __, __, __

155. 1, 4, 3, 6, 5, __, __, __, __

156. 1, 2, 3, 6, 7, 14, 15, __, __, __, __

157. 1, 2, 4, 7, 11, __, __, __, __

158. 1, 3, 4, 12, 13, __, __, __, __

Reference

*Basic
Thinking
Skills*

*Mind
Benders®
A1–A4*

MIND BENDERS®

PROBLEMS

159. Samisoni and Germaine each have two jobs. The jobs are dentist, carpenter, electrician, and house cleaner.

The dentist doesn't know a ground wire from a live wire.

Samisoni is not the carpenter.

Germaine is not the dentist.

Find each person's two jobs.

In Michigan, you are never more than six miles from a lake or a stream.

Reference

Taken from Basic Thinking Skills

160. THE TRUTH-TELLERS AND THE LIARS

The people on a certain island are divided into two groups—the truth-tellers and the liars.

The truth-tellers always tell the truth.

The liars always lie.

There are no half-truths or half-lies.

A stranger comes to the island one day and sees three of the natives standing together.

The first native says, "I am not a liar." The second native says, "He's lying." The third native says, "They're both lying."

What is the third native—a truth-teller or a liar? Explain your answer.

Reference

Taken from Basic Thinking Skills

FANTASY OR TRUE TO LIFE?

DIRECTIONS

A few statements are given to start a story. Accept these statements as true.

These statements are followed by some lettered statements.

Decide whether the lettered statements sound true to life, or whether they sound more like fantasy.

EXAMPLE

Problem:

Diane had a very intelligent cat named Tiger. Diane taught Tiger to walk for a short distance on his hind legs. She also taught him to sit up and to shake hands.

a. Tiger could tell from the way Diane acted that she disliked his sharpening his claws on the furniture, so he stopped doing that and instead sharpened his claws on a tree when Diane let him go outside.

b. Tiger got bored with playing with a ball of string, so he found Diane's crochet hook and crocheted a small doily from the string.

Answer:

a. true to life

b. fantasy

Reference

Basic
Thinking
Skills

PROBLEMS

161. Ropata, who is twelve years old, was the best first baseman and the best batter in his baseball little league.

One day he came home from practice and his father told him, "Your coach just now telephoned. He said to tell you that the

a. All-Star Selection Committee has chosen you to be one of the players on the Little League All-Star team."

b. principal of your school said that you're going to have to drop out of the Little League if your school grades don't start improving."

c. manager of the Cincinnati Reds wants us to fly in to see him tomorrow so that you can sign a contract to play for them."

Reference

Basic
Thinking
Skills

d. bat you cracked when you hit that foul ball in yesterday's game has been examined and found to be defective. The committee ruled that the foul ball should have been a home run, and so yesterday's game will be replayed, starting from that point."

e. National Baseball Hall of Fame in Cooperstown has waived its usual rules for membership, and you've been elected to the Hall of Fame."

f. baseball coach at Stanford University wants you to enroll at Stanford and start playing baseball there next year."

g. publicity you've been getting has gone to your head, and he's going to start keeping you on the bench if you don't stop acting so conceited about it."

Reference

Basic
Thinking
Skills

162. Laura didn't understand today's arithmetic lesson.

The teacher had already said what they were going to study tomorrow, and Laura didn't see how she could understand that if she didn't understand today's lesson, so she

a. stayed after school to get extra help from the teacher, and then she understood the lesson.

b. asked her big brother for help with it, but she still didn't understand the lesson when he was through explaining it to her.

c. told her dog, King, about it and showed him her arithmetic book. King read the material and then explained it to Laura so that she understood it.

Reference

Basic Thinking Skills

d. said, "Oh, I wish some good angel would appear and explain it to me!" A good angel appeared and explained it to her, and Laura understood the lesson.

e. said, "Oh, I wish I had a fairy godmother who'd make me smart enough to understand this!" But no fairy godmother appeared, and Laura still didn't understand the lesson when she went back to school the next day.

f. gave up trying to understand it. She picked numbers out of thin air for the answers to the fifteen homework problems, and when the homework was checked in class the next day, every one of Laura's answers turned out to be right.

g. concentrated very hard the next day on the new lesson, and she understood every bit of it, even though she still didn't understand the previous lesson, and even though the new lesson was based on the previous lesson.

CLOCK ARITHMETIC

LESSON

We all do clock arithmetic. We say things like "an hour ago" or "three hours from now."

If it is now 9 o'clock, then "an hour ago" means 8 o'clock, and "three hours from now" means 12 o'clock.

When we have to count past 12 o'clock, we start at 1 o'clock again. If it is 11 o'clock now, then "three hours from now" means 2 o'clock.

DIRECTIONS

You are told what time it is now. You are asked to find a different time.

EXAMPLE

Problem: 7 o'clock; 2 hours from now

Answer: 9 o'clock

PROBLEMS

163. 7 o'clock; 2 hours ago

164. 7 o'clock; 5 hours from now

165. 9 o'clock; 5 hours from now

166. 11 o'clock; 4 hours from now

167. 12 o'clock; 8 hours ago

168. 4 o'clock; 7 hours ago

169. 10 o'clock; 6 hours from now

170. 3 o'clock; 10 hours ago

LESSON CONT.

Suppose we had a clock that went only from 1 to 8 instead of from 1 to 12.

We could do the same kind of arithmetic with it that we do for a 12-hour clock.

With a 12-hour clock, we count from 1 to 12 and then start over.

With an 8-hour clock, we would count from 1 to 8 and then start over.

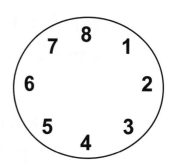

EXAMPLE 1

Suppose it is 5 o'clock now.

Then 3 hours from now it will be 8 o'clock, and 4 hours from now it will be 1 o'clock.

EXAMPLE 2

Suppose it is 2 o'clock now.

Then 2 hours ago it was 8 o'clock, and 3 hours ago it was 7 o'clock.

DIRECTIONS

You are told what time it is now. You are asked to find a different time.

Use an 8-hour clock.

EXAMPLE

Problem: 7 o'clock; 2 hours from now
Answer: 1 o'clock

PROBLEMS

171. 7 o'clock; 3 hours from now

172. 3 o'clock; 3 hours ago

173. 6 o'clock; 8 hours from now

174. 6 o'clock; 8 hours ago

175. 5 o'clock; 6 hours from now

176. 4 o'clock; 9 hours from now

> **DIRECTIONS**
>
> Now try analogous ideas on other clocks.

EXAMPLE 1

Problem: 6-hour clock; now 5 o'clock; 3 hours from now
Answer: 2 o'clock

PROBLEMS

177. 6-hour clock; now 5 o'clock; 7 hours from now

178. 7-hour clock; now 2 o'clock; 5 hours ago

179. 10-hour clock; now 8 o'clock; 7 hours from now

180. 4-hour clock; now 3 o'clock; 3 hours from now

181. 9-hour clock; now 4 o'clock; 15 hours from now

182. 9-hour clock; now 2 o'clock; 24 hours ago

183. 3-hour clock; now 1 o'clock; 14 hours from now

184. 3-hour clock; now 1 o'clock; 14 hours ago

185. 5-hour clock; now 3 o'clock; 10 hours ago

186. 7-hour clock; now 6 o'clock; 9 hours from now

187. 4-hour clock; now 2 o'clock; 7 hours from now

188. 10-hour clock; now 7 o'clock; 11 hours ago

189. MARIO'S METHOD FOR CLOCK ARITHMETIC

Mario says he has a fast way of doing clock arithmetic. He gave these examples:

"Suppose it's a 6-hour clock. If my answer is more than 6, I subtract 6. If it's going to be less than 1, I add 6. Say it's 4 o'clock and I want 5 hours from now. I take 4 + 5 and get 9. That's more than 6, so I subtract 6 and get 3, so the answer is 3 o'clock.

"Or say it's 1 o'clock and I want 3 hours ago. If I take 1 – 3, I'll get less than 1, so I add 6 first. I take 6 + 1 – 3 and get 4, so the answer is 4 o'clock."

Julia asked what happens if his answer is still more than 6 for a 6-hour clock. He said he keeps subtracting 6s until the answer is between 1 and 6. Julia used Mario's method to find the time 8 hours after 5 o'clock. She took 8 + 5 – 6 – 6 and got 1 o'clock, and that answer is correct.

Loretta asked Mario what he does for a 6-hour clock if the problem says to find the time 16 hours ago if it's 2 o'clock now. He said he keeps adding 6s to the 2 until he gets a number more than 16, and then he subtracts.

a. Do you think Mario's method will *always* work for a 6-hour clock? If so, how come? If not, give a counterexample.

b. 1) What would Mario's method be for a 9-hour clock?

  2) Do you think his method will work for a 9-hour clock? If so, how come? If not, give a counterexample.

c. Do you think Mario's method will work for other clocks? If so, how come? If not, give a counterexample.

190. CHOON-WEI'S METHOD FOR CLOCK ARITHMETIC

Choon-Wei said she has a fast method for doing clock arithmetic, too.

For a 6-hour clock, she does the same as Mario if the hours to be added or subtracted are less than 6. But if those hours are more than 6, she subtracts 6s right away.

Choon-Wei gave these examples:

"Say it's 3 o'clock now and I want to know the time 14 hours from now. I take 14 − 6 − 6 and get 2, and then I add that to 3 and get 5, so it will be 5 o'clock then.

"Or say it's 3 o'clock now and I want the time 14 hours ago. I take 14 − 6 − 6 and get 2, and I subtract that from 3 and get 1, so it was 1 o'clock then."

Larry said her method wouldn't work for a problem like 14 hours ago if it's 1 o'clock now, because 14 − 6 − 6 is 2, and 1 − 2 is less than 1. Choon-Wei said he was wrong, because his example reduced the problem to finding the time 2 hours ago if it's 1 o'clock now, and she already said that she uses Mario's method for that kind of problem.

a. Do you think Choon-Wei's method will *always* work for a 6-hour clock? If so, how come? If not, give a counterexample.

b. Suppose Choon-Wei uses analogous reasoning for a 7-hour clock. How would she find the time 15 hours from now if it is now 2 o'clock?

c. Do you think Choon-Wei's method will work for other clocks? If so, how come? If not, give a counterexample.

LESSON CONT.

We have used clock arithmetic on
different clocks and found that the
arithmetic is analogous for all clocks.

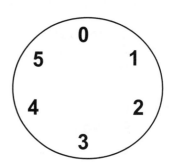

Now think about a 6-hour clock whose
6 has been replaced with 0. The clock
will still have 6 numbers, but they will
go from 0 through 5 instead of from 1
through 6.

Suppose it is now 1 o'clock. Then 5
hours from now it should be 6 o'clock.
But our clock has 0 instead of 6, so it will
be 0 o'clock.

We will work problems the same way we would work them if the clock's
numbers were 1 through 6. There will be no change unless we get a final
answer of 6, in which case our answer will be 0 instead.

EXAMPLES

Problem: Find the time 3 hours after 5 o'clock.

Solution: 5 + 3 = 8. The clock numbers don't go that far, so we subtract
6 and get 8 − 6 = 2.

Answer: 2 o'clock

Problem: Find the time 14 hours after 4 o'clock.

Solution: 4 + 14 = 18. That's too much, so subtract 6. 18 − 6 = 12.
That's still too much, so subtract another 6. 12 − 6 = 6. Our
clock doesn't go up to 6, so we subtract another 6. 6 − 6 = 0.

Answer: 0 o'clock

Problem: Find the time 7 hours before 3 o'clock.

Solution: 3 − 7 is less than 0, so we will add 6. We will get 6 + 3 − 7 =
9 − 7 = 2.

Answer: 2 o'clock

DIRECTIONS

You have a 6-hour clock whose numbers run from 0 through 5.

You are asked to find the time some number of hours before or after a given starting time.

EXAMPLE

Problem: Now 4 o'clock; 7 hours later

Solution: 4 + 7 = 11; 11 − 6 = 5

Answer: 5 o'clock

PROBLEMS

191. Now 1 o'clock; 7 hours later

192. Now 3 o'clock; 5 hours earlier

193. Now 5 o'clock; 13 hours later

194. Now 0 o'clock; 11 hours later

195. Now 2 o'clock; 10 hours earlier

196. Now 4 o'clock; 20 hours from now

197. Now 4 o'clock; 20 hours ago

OTHER BASES

LESSON

Think about the way we write numbers. We start with only ten digits:

0   1   2   3   4   5   6   7   8   9

The first digit, 0, is for zero. After that, they mean 0 + 1, 0 + 2, 0 + 3, and so on, up through 0 + 9.

We don't invent new digits when we want to write a number past 9. Instead, we use what we already have, but we write them side by side:

10   11   12   13   14   15   16   17   18   19

Notice that this row of numbers is exactly like the top row, except that each number in this row starts with 1. This 1 means that we've used all ten of our digits once before, and we've started over again.

The first symbol here, 10, is for ten because we had ten digits. After that, they mean 10 + 1, 10 + 2, 10 + 3, and so on, up through 10 + 9.

After we've written 19, we've used our ten digits twice apiece, so each number in the next row starts with 2:

20   21   22   23   24   25   26   27   28   29

The first symbol here, 20, is for two tens, 2×10. After that, they mean $(2 \times 10) + 1$, $(2 \times 10) + 2$, $(2 \times 10) + 3$, and so on, up through $(2 \times 10) + 9$.

We keep going the same way up through the 90s:

90   91   92   93   94   95   96   97   98   99

This time the first symbol, 90, is for nine tens, 9×10. The others mean $(9 \times 10) + 1$, $(9 \times 10) + 2$, $(9 \times 10) + 3$, and so on, up through $(9 \times 10) + 9$.

When we reached 90, we had used all ten of our digits 9 times before. Now that we've written 99, we've used all ten digits 10 times, and we have no digits left to write a higher number.

We had an analogous problem after we wrote the number 9. We had used all ten digits once and had to think of a way to write ten, the next number after nine.

We solved that problem by starting at 0 again but writing 1 to the left of 0 to show that the ten digits had all been used one time before.

We will solve this problem in an analogous way. We'll start at 0 again but write 10 to the left of it to show that we've used all ten digits ten times: $100 = 10 \times 10$.

To be more exact, 100 really means

$$1 \times (10 \times 10) \quad + \quad 0 \times 10 \quad + \quad 0 \times 1.$$

Here are some other examples:

$$205 = 2 \times (10 \times 10) \quad + \quad 0 \times 10 \quad + \quad 5 \times 1$$

$$359 = 3 \times (10 \times 10) \quad + \quad 5 \times 10 \quad + \quad 9 \times 1$$

Notice that we write numbers in a special way:

The last digit (on the right) tells how many 1s there are.

$$7 = 7 \times 1$$

The digit to the left of it tells how many 10s there are.

$$37 = 3 \times 10 \quad + \quad 7 \times 1$$

The digit to the left of that one tells how many (10×10)s there are.

$$637 = 6 \times (10 \times 10) \quad + \quad 3 \times 10 \quad + 7 \times 1$$

DIRECTIONS

Write each number in expanded form.

EXAMPLE

Problem: 352

Answer: $352 = 3 \times (10 \times 10) + 5 \times 10 + 2 \times 1$

PROBLEMS

198. 38

199. 70

200. 99

201. 506

202. 480

203. 217

204. 3145 (I know this wasn't in the lesson, but take a guess.)

LESSON CONT.

Because we use ten different digits to write numbers, we say that we use a *base* of ten to write them, or that we write them in *base ten*.

Look at 637 again. Each place held by a digit means something different. Going from right to left, the first digit is in the 1s place, the second digit is in the 10s place, and the third digit is in the (10 × 10)s place.

For a four-digit number, the fourth digit would be in the (10 × 10 × 10)s place, and so on.

Now suppose we didn't have ten different digits. Suppose there were only five different digits—0, 1, 2, 3, and 4. Then we would write the numbers in base five.

34 in base five = (in either base five or base ten) 3 × 5 + 4 = (in base ten) 15 + 4 = 19.

Notice that we don't write "34 = 19," because that wouldn't make sense. Neither can we write "base 5" (because there is no 5 in base five) or "base 10" (because 10 means different things in different bases).

We could show the base by subscripts:
$$34_{five} = (3 \times 5 + 4)_{ten} = (15 + 4)_{ten} = 19_{ten}.$$

Or we could use columns:

Base five	Base ten
34	3 × 5 + 4 = 15 + 4 = 19
201	2 × (5 × 5) + 0 × 5 + 1 × 1 = 50 + 0 + 1 = 51
37	Cannot convert. There is no 7 in base five.

205. Write the numbers from one through sixteen in base five.

206. Write the numbers from one through nineteen in base six.

207. Write the numbers from one through twenty-two in base seven.

208. Write the numbers from one through twenty-five in base eight.

209. In the problems above, the last base ten numbers were 16, 19, 22, 25. For the first three of these, notice the difference between each number and the next one.

You should see that this difference has something to do with the last number you wrote for each of the four problems.

a. Suppose you were to write two lists of numbers, one in base ninety-six* and the other in base ninety-seven, starting at 1 and ending at $81_{\text{ninety-six}}$ and $81_{\text{ninety-seven}}$. In base ten, these last numbers would not be the same.

Without converting $81_{\text{ninety-six}}$ and $81_{\text{ninety-seven}}$ to base ten, tell what would be the difference in base ten between these two numbers, and tell how you know.

b. Same question as for part a, except the last numbers were $85_{\text{ninety-six}}$ and $85_{\text{ninety-seven}}$.

_____

* We'd have to use different symbols to count past 9. For bases through base thirty-six, capital block letters are used. Example:

base ten: 1 2 3 4 5 6 7 8 9 10 11 12 13 14 15
base twelve: 1 2 3 4 5 6 7 8 9 A B 10 11 12 13

DIRECTIONS

You are given a number written in base five. Convert it to a base ten number.

EXAMPLE

Problem: 123

Answer: 123_{five} = (in base ten) $1 \times (5 \times 5) + 2 \times 5 + 3 \times 1 = 25 + 10 + 3 = 38$

PROBLEMS

210. 21

211. 44

212. 132

213. 420

214. 1000

215. 1020

216. Think about how you add numbers in base ten. For example, to do this problem

$$247$$
$$+\ 56$$

you start by adding 7 and 6. You get 13, which can't all go in the 1s column, so you enter 3 in the 1s column and carry the other 10 to the 10s column.

$$1$$
$$247$$
$$+\ 56$$
$$3$$

That's 1 ten you've carried there, so that column now has (1 + 4 + 5) tens = 10 tens. You can't put 10 in one column, so you enter 0 there and carry the other 10 to the next column.

$$11$$
$$247$$
$$+\ \ 56$$
$$03$$

That's 1 ten × ten you've carried there, so that column now has (1 + 2) ten × tens = 3 ten × tens.

$$11$$
$$247$$
$$+\ 56$$
$$303$$

All right, so now that we've reviewed that, see if you can use analogous reasoning to figure out how to add in base five. Here's how to go about it:

Make up some base five addition problems.

When you get an answer to each problem, convert the problem and the answer to base ten.

Check the addition in base ten to make sure that your answer is right.

Reference

Algebra
Word
Problems—
Diophan-
tine
Problems

Classroom
Quickies—
Books 1–3

DIOPHANTINE PROBLEMS

PROBLEM

217. Jonathan has lost all of his marbles to Eunice again, and he has heard about another sale.

He wants to buy 100 marbles for $1 again.

How many of each can he get if shooters are 5¢ each, red marbles are 3¢ each, and multicolored marbles are 3 for a penny?

(Hint: There is more than one answer to this problem.)

If a rooster flies up to the peak of a roof and lays an egg exactly at dawn, which way does the egg roll—to the right or to the left?

Reference

*Classroom
Quickies—
Books 1–3*

REARRANGE LETTERS

DIRECTIONS

Use the letters at the top to fill in the chart so that words are formed and the sentence makes sense.

- A shaded space in the chart shows the end of a word.

- Except for the last line, the end of a line is not the end of a word unless there is a shaded space there.

- When you have filled in the chart, answer the question asked.

PROBLEM

218.

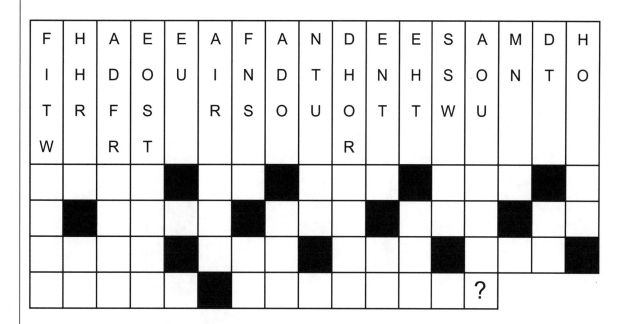

Reference

Classroom Quickies— Books 1–3

WATER JUGS PROBLEMS

PROBLEM

219. You have three jugs and a river of clean water. The jugs are known to hold exactly 5, 7, and 11 liters.

Tell how you can use these jugs to measure exactly 6 liters of water.

Where does the light go when you turn off the switch?

Reference

Classroom Quickies— Book 2

MISCELLANEOUS PROBLEMS

PROBLEMS

220. Jody, who is colorblind, has a black pen, a blue pen, and a red pen.

His sister Nina wrote the name of each color on a label and attached the label to the pen so that he would know its color.

His little brother, Cameron, was playing around with the pens and Nina told Jody that Cameron had mixed up all of the labels.

Jody thought about this and then decided that if Nina would tell him the correct color of just one of the pens, he could figure out how to relabel all three pens correctly.

How could he do this?

Reference

Algebra
Word
Problems—
Miscellan-
eous A-1

Math
Word
Problems

221. If a cow costs $300, how much will a gallon of milk at 70¢ a quart cost?

222. A half-liter bottle of orange juice, plus the bottle deposit, came to a total of 60¢.

The orange juice was 40¢ more than the bottle deposit.

How much was the

a. orange juice?

b. bottle deposit?

WEIGHING BALLS

PROBLEM

223. You have five balls, all of which look exactly the same.

Four of them all weigh the same, and the fifth one is known to be slightly lighter.

You have a balance scale. How can you find the odd ball in at most two weighings?

ANALOGIES IN PROPORTIONS

LESSON

A fraction is a ratio (RAY sho or RAY she o).

A true statement that two ratios are equal is a *proportion* (pruh POR shun).

We say that two equal ratios are *proportional* or *in proportion* to each other.

EXAMPLE 1

These are ratos:

$$\frac{1}{2} \quad \frac{5}{3} \quad \frac{10}{11}$$

These are proportions:

$$\frac{2}{1} = \frac{3}{6} \qquad \frac{2}{1} = \frac{6}{3} \qquad \frac{20}{40} = \frac{40}{60}$$

These are proportional, and they are in proportion to each other

$$\frac{2}{1} \text{ and } \frac{10}{5} \qquad \frac{3}{5} \text{ and } \frac{6}{10}$$

A proportion can be stated as an analogy.

EXAMPLE 2

$$\frac{1}{2} = \frac{3}{6},$$ so 1 is to 2 as 3 is to 6.

Notice that an analogy uses "is to" instead of a fraction bar (—) and uses "as" instead of an equal sign (=). So, given the proportion

$$\frac{2}{4} = \frac{5}{10},$$

an analogy reads it as

2 is to 4 as 5 is to 10

instead of

two fourths equals five tenths

and instead of

2 divided by 4 equals 5 divided by 10.

DIRECTIONS

You are given four numbers. Tell whether or not they can be used to form a proportion. If they can, then use them to write at least three different proportions. Also state each proportion as an analogy.

EXAMPLE 1

Problem: 4, 5, 2, 10

Answer: Yes.

$$\frac{4}{2} = \frac{10}{5};$$ 4 is to 2 as 10 is to 5

$$\frac{2}{5} = \frac{4}{10};$$ 2 is to 5 as 4 is to 10

$$\frac{2}{4} = \frac{5}{10};$$ 2 is to 4 as 5 is to 10

(There are also five other proportions that can be made from these four numbers.)

EXAMPLE 2

Problem: 1, 5, 2, 8

Answer: No

PROBLEMS

224. 1, 5, 2, 10

225. 2, 5, 4, 7

226. 2, 4, 2, 1

227. 1, 8, 3, 24

228. 2, 18, 9, 4

229. 2, 4, 1, 6

230. 3, 8, 6, 4

231. 10, 12, 15, 8

Hints for Problems on Pages 108–122

If a problem talks about a common factor, assume that this factor is not 1.

Also assume that all numbers are greater than zero.

If you are not given any numbers, find numbers of your own to use. See how they relate to each other or what happens to them when you do what the problem says.

Then choose another set of numbers. See if they relate to each other or act in the same way as the first numbers did.

Keep choosing numbers until you can *predict* what they have to be like or what will happen to them in the problem. (Or maybe you feel that *no* numbers will work.) Figure out how to prove that your reasoning would apply no matter which (allowable) numbers were chosen.

You are allowed to use anything already proved. For example, if you are doing problem 238 and need a statement proved in problem 233, then you may use it without proving it again.

To help yourself imagine a general proportion, make a set of fraction bars and an equal sign

$$\underline{\qquad} = \underline{\qquad}$$

and fill in the four terms with four different geometric figures—say, a circle, a square, a triangle, and a rhombus:

$$\frac{\bigcirc}{\square} = \frac{\triangle}{\diamondsuit}$$

Then you'll have something to stare at while you're trying to figure out how to solve the problem.

232. Someone is thinking of a proportion.

Three of the four numbers are the same.

What, if anything, can you tell about the remaining number without actually seeing the proportion? How come?

233. You are given a proportion. Explain why you can switch the two ratios (to the opposite sides of the equation) and still have a proportion.

234. You are given four numbers.

For each of the special conditions a, b, and c below, tell whether or not it is possible to arrange the four numbers to form a proportion. In each case,

A. if a proportion is possible, give an example of such a proportion. You are allowed to use any numbers you choose for this.

B. if a proportion is not possible, tell why not.

EXAMPLE

Special condition: One of the numbers is five more than another of the numbers.

Answer Yes. $\dfrac{1}{6} = \dfrac{2}{12}$ (Other proportions are possible.)

Special conditions for the problem

   a. Two of the numbers are the same and the other two are different.

   b. No two of the numbers are the same.

   c. One of the numbers is 2 more than another; a third number is 3 more than the remaining number.

Here is a list of some of the problems proved. If a statement says you can do something to a proportion, then you will still have a proportion afterwards. In this list, GAP = Given a proportion.

232. GAP, if three of the terms are equal, then the fourth term is equal, too.

233. GAP, you can switch the two ratios.

235. You are given a proportion with four distinct terms.

Which of the terms can you not switch with each other and still end up with a proportion?

(Hint: To prove that something cannot always be done, all you have to do is come up with a counterexample.)

Here is a list of some of the problems proved. If a statement says you can do something to a proportion, then you will still have a proportion afterwards. In this list, GAP = Given a proportion.

232. GAP, if three of the terms are equal, then the fourth term is equal, too.

233. GAP, you can switch the two ratios.

236. You are given the numbers 1, 5, and 8.

a. Find a fourth number such that all four numbers can be used as the terms of a proportion.

b. Write the proportion.

237. You are given some numbers that can be organized into a proportion.

Tell how many different proportions are possible, and give an example of such a proportion, if

a. two of the numbers are the same, and the other two are different from those but the same as each other.

b. two of the numbers are the same, and the other two are different from those and from each other.

c. the four numbers are distinct.

Here is a list of some of the problems proved. If a statement says you can do something to a proportion, then you will still have a proportion afterwards. In this list, GAP = Given a proportion.

232. GAP, if three of the terms are equal, then the fourth term is equal, too.

233. GAP, you can switch the two ratios.

238. You are given a proportion. Tell why

a. if the numerators are equal, then the denominators are equal.

b. if the denominators are equal, then the numerators are equal.

Here is a list of some of the problems proved. If a statement says you can do something to a proportion, then you will still have a proportion afterwards. In this list, GAP = Given a proportion.

233. GAP, you can switch the two ratios.

238. GAP: if the numerators are =, then the denominators are =; and if the denominators are =, then the numerators are =.

239. You are given a proportion.

One of its ratios has two unequal terms.

Tell why the terms of the other ratio also have to be unequal.

Here is a list of some of the problems proved. If a statement says you can do something to a proportion, then you will still have a proportion afterwards. In this list, GAP = Given a proportion.

233. GAP, you can switch the two ratios.

238. GAP: if the numerators are =, then the denominators are =; and if the denominators are =, then the numerators are =.

240. A proportion always looks like this:

$$\frac{\text{first term}}{\text{second term}} = \frac{\text{third term}}{\text{fourth term}}$$

The first and fourth terms are called the *extremes*, or the outer terms, of the proportion.

The second and third terms are called the *means*, or the inner terms, of the proportion.

In a proportion, the product of the extremes always equals the product of the means. How come?

Here are two other ways to state what you are to explain:

first term × fourth term = second term × third term

product of outer terms = product of inner terms

Here is a list of some of the problems proved. If a statement says you can do something to a proportion, then you will still have a proportion afterwards. In this list, GAP = Given a proportion.

233. GAP, you can switch the two ratios.

238. GAP: if the numerators are =, then the denominators are =; and if the denominators are =, then the numerators are =.

240. GAP, the product of the extremes = the product of the means.

241. You are given that the product of two numbers equals the product of two other numbers. (For example, $3 \times 4 = 2 \times 6$.)

Explain why a proportion will be formed if you use one pair of numbers as the extremes and you use the other pair as the means.

EXAMPLE

Given $3 \times 4 = 2 \times 6$, suppose you choose 3 and 4 to be the extremes. Then 2 and 6 will be the means, and the proportion could look like this:

$$\frac{3}{2} = \frac{6}{4}$$

(Hint: You are given an equation. Remember that both sides of an equation can be divided by the same number.)

Here is a list of some of the problems proved. If a statement says you can do something to a proportion, then you will still have a proportion afterwards. In this list, GAP = Given a proportion.

233. GAP, you can switch the two ratios.

238. GAP: if the numerators are =, then the denominators are =; and if the denominators are =, then the numerators are =.

240. GAP, the product of the extremes = the product of the means.

241. If the product of two numbers = the product of two numbers, then one pair may be made the extremes of a proportion, and the other pair will be the means.

242. You are given a proportion.

Prove that you will still have a proportion if you switch

a. the means of the given proportion.

b. the extremes of the given proportion.

(Note: Each new proportion will be different from the one you started with.)

Here is a list of some of the problems proved. If a statement says you can do something to a proportion, then you will still have a proportion afterwards. In this list, GAP = Given a proportion.

233. GAP, you can switch the two ratios.

238. GAP: if the numerators are =, then the denominators are =; and if the denominators are =, then the numerators are =.

240. GAP, the product of the extremes = the product of the means.

241–242. If the product of two numbers = the product of two numbers, then either pair may be made the extremes of a proportion, and the other pair will be the means.

243. If you invert both of a proportion's ratios (turn them both upside down), will the result still be a proportion? How come?

(Hint: Use problems 240 and 241–242.)

Here is a list of some of the problems proved. If a statement says you can do something to a proportion, then you will still have a proportion afterwards. In this list, GAP = Given a proportion.

238. GAP: if the numerators are =, then the denominators are =; and if the denominators are =, then the numerators are =.

240. GAP, the product of the extremes = the product of the means.

241–242. If the product of two numbers = the product of two numbers, then either pair may be made the extremes of a proportion, and the other pair will be the means.

244. You are given four numbers that will be terms of a proportion if you can place them correctly.

Tell why a proportion can be formed no matter which one of the four numbers you use as the first term, if

a. three of the numbers are the same.

b. two of the numbers are the same, and the other two numbers are

1) the same as each other but different from the first two.

2) different from each other and from the first two.

Here is a list of some of the problems proved. If a statement says you can do something to a proportion, then you will still have a proportion afterwards. In this list, GAP = Given a proportion.

238. GAP: if the numerators are =, then the denominators are =; and if the denominators are =, then the numerators are =.

240. GAP, the product of the extremes = the product of the means.

241–242. If the product of two numbers = the product of two numbers, then either pair may be made the extremes of a proportion, and the other pair will be the means.

243. GAP, you can invert both ratios.

245. You are given four distinct numbers that can be the four terms of a proportion.

Prove that the numbers can be sorted in at least one way so that a proportion is *not* formed.

246. You are given the numbers 1, 5, and 8 to be used as three terms of a proportion, not necessarily consecutively.

a. How many different fourth numbers are possible to use for the other term? What are these numbers?

b. Once a fourth number is chosen, how many different proportions can be made from the four numbers?

Here is a list of some of the problems proved. If a statement says you can do something to a proportion, then you will still have a proportion afterwards. In this list, GAP = Given a proportion.

238. GAP: if the numerators are =, then the denominators are =; and if the denominators are =, then the numerators are =.

240. GAP, the product of the extremes = the product of the means.

241–242. If the product of two numbers = the product of two numbers, then either pair may be made the extremes of a proportion, and the other pair will be the means.

243. GAP, you can invert both ratios.

247. You are given a proportion with four distinct terms, all of which are whole numbers.

Explain why at least two of the terms have to have a common factor.

(Hint: Remember that you can multiply both sides of an equation by the same number.)

Reference

Classroom
Quickies—
Books 1–3

REARRANGE LETTERS

DIRECTIONS

Use the letters at the top to fill in the chart so that words are formed and the sentence makes sense.

- A shaded space in the chart shows the end of a word.

- Except for the last line, the end of a line is not the end of a word unless there is a shaded space there.

- When you have filled in the chart, answer the question asked.

PROBLEM

248.

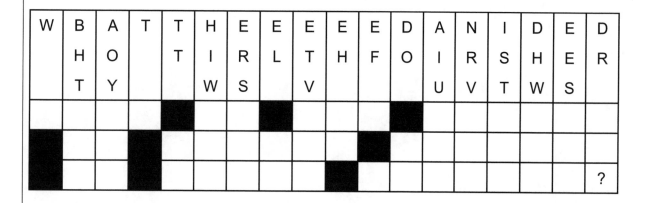

Reference

Classroom Quickies— Books 1–3

WATER JUGS PROBLEMS

PROBLEM

249. You have three jugs and a river of clean water.

The jugs are known to hold exactly 5, 7, and 11 gallons.

Tell how you can use these jugs to measure exactly 8 gallons of water.

This is a simple subtraction problem. Six cats were glaring at each other and yowling outside the kitchen door of a high-class restaurant. One of them got soaked and ran away when the chef threw a pan of water at them. How many cats remained?

Reference

Algebra Word Problems— Diophantine Problems

Classroom Quickies— Books 1–3

DIOPHANTINE PROBLEMS

PROBLEM

250. Well, Jonathan is improving at playing marbles, but so is Eunice, and Jonathan has lost his marbles to Eunice again.

He is going to another sale and will buy 100 marbles for $1, just as he did before, but this time the prices are 3¢ each for shooters, 2¢ each for red marbles, and 2 for a penny for multicolored marbles.

How many of each kind of marble can he get?

A group of birds is called a flock of birds. What is a group of lions called?

Reference

Math
Word
Problems

MISCELLANEOUS PROBLEMS

PROBLEM

251. If you write down for your answer 25 more than the correct answer, what do you write down for your answer to

a. $14 + 9 = ?$

b. $11 \times 11 = ?$

c. $17 + 15 - 6 = ?$

d. $2 \times 4 \times 7 = ?$

e. $6 \times 10 \div 4 = ?$

f. $13 + 15 - 4 + 6 = ?$

Reference

*Inductive
Thinking
Skills*

RELEVANT INFORMATION

LESSON

Suppose you are thinking about whether or not to get your hair cut.

You tell your friend James, and he makes a comment.

If his comment is supposed to help you reach a decision, then his comment is *relevant* (REL uh vuhnt). Otherwise, his comment is irrelevant or not relevant.

EXAMPLE

Problem: Should you get your hair cut or not?

Relevant comments from James:

You look better with your hair as it is now.

Will you have enough money to pay for it?

Your hair is too long now.

Your hair isn't long enough now.

Irrelevant comments, or comments that are not relevant:

My brother got his hair cut yesterday.

You have brown eyes.

My mother always cuts my hair.

You got your hair cut two weeks ago, didn't you?

We say that a statement (or question) is relevant to a subject if that statement (or question) has a bearing upon the subject.

A relevant statement (or question) always has a logical connection with the subject.

Reference

Inductive Thinking Skills

DIRECTIONS

A problem is stated and is followed by several lettered sentences.

For each lettered sentence, tell whether or not it is relevant to the problem.

PROBLEM

252. Ms. Brown is a secretary in a large office and wants to change her job. A friend told her that she should consider being a teacher in an elementary school.

Some people think she would be a good teacher, but other people think she would not.

Decide which of the following statements are relevant to whether or not she would be a good teacher.

a. She is not good at explaining things.

b. She is good at explaining things.

c. She has blue eyes.

d. She has not gone to college.

e. She likes to learn new things.

f. She likes children.

g. She does not like children.

h. She lives too far away to teach here at this school.

i. She doesn't like it when someone questions what she says.

j. She isn't intelligent enough to be a good teacher.

Reference

*Inductive
Thinking
Skills*

k.   I don't like her.

l.   The salary for teaching isn't too bad.

m.   She doesn't understand children.

n.   Being a secretary is nothing like being a teacher.

o.   Most people these days have more than one career in their
lifetime, so there's no reason she shouldn't try being a teacher.

p.   She's too old to be a good teacher.

Reference

*Inductive
Thinking
Skills*

DIRECTIONS

A problem is stated and is followed by several lettered sentences.

For each lettered sentence, tell whether or not it is relevant to the problem.

PROBLEM

253. Jessica is going with her parents to visit her grandparents this evening.

She wants to do her homework, but even if she does some homework before the visit and some when she gets home again, she will not be able to do all of it before she gets too tired to concentrate.

a. She could do the hard parts before and after the visit and take the easy parts with her to do during the visit.

b. I'd just do what I could and not worry about the rest.

c. Jessica's grades are good enough so that she doesn't have to worry about missing one homework assignment.

d. Is all the homework due tomorrow?

Reference

*Inductive
Thinking
Skills*

e. Does she have a study period at school before some of the homework is due?

f. Are they going to take their dog with them when they visit?

g. Maybe she could get up earlier than usual and finish it tomorrow morning.

h. It doesn't matter whether or not she does it, because most of it is just busywork, anyhow.

i. She could get her big sister to do some of it for her.

j. She could look through all of it and not bother writing out the answers she's sure of. Then she could spend the time she has looking up the other answers. That way, she'd get it all done.

Reference

Inductive Thinking Skills

DIRECTIONS

A problem is stated and is followed by several lettered sentences.

For each lettered sentence, tell whether or not it is relevant to the problem.

PROBLEM

254. Carlyle says he has trouble remembering simple multiplication facts such as how much 7 × 3 is.

He asked his friends how he could learn to remember such facts.

Here are some comments made by some of his friends.

a. You could make a multiplication table and study it.

b. You don't have to remember them. Just write down seven 3's and add them up.

c. At first, I had trouble remembering them, too.

d. Try learning just three of them each day. Say them over and over. The next day, say the ones you've already learned and then learn three more.

e. My little sister knows them already, and she's a year younger than I am.

f. Write a whole page of just one of the facts. By the time you finish, you should remember that one. Then do a whole page of another one.

g. Make a set of flash cards for all of the facts, but use only four or five of the cards while you drill yourself on them for about ten minutes. Then use a different set of four or five for another ten minutes.

h. Sharon has trouble with them, too, but she isn't worrying about it.

i. I went to a circus last year and saw a horse that could multiply. Someone would call out a problem, and the horse would go to a row of answer cards and pick out the right answer.

Reference

*Algebra
Word
Problems–
How to
Solve
Algebra
Word
Problems*

*Math Word
Problems*

TEMPERATURE SCALES

LESSON

The two temperature scales most often used in the U.S. are the *Fahrenheit* (FAIR un hyt) scale and the *Celsius* (SELL see us) scale.

Furnace thermostats usually show Fahrenheit degrees.

Both Fahrenheit and Celsius degrees often appear on outdoor thermometers.

Thermometers used by hospitals to take body temperatures usually show Celsius degrees.

Scientific standards use Celsius degrees.

Fahrenheit numbers are higher than Celsius numbers. As a very rough way to go from Celsius to Fahrenheit, you can double the Celsius number and add 25 or 30.

Similarly, a rough way to go from Fahrenheit to Celsius is to subtract 25 or 30 from the Fahrenheit number and then take half of the result.

The correct way to go from Celsius to Fahrenheit is to double the number, subtract $\frac{1}{10}$ of what you get, and then add 32.

EXAMPLE 1

Problem: Convert 5° Celsius to Fahrenheit.
Solution: Double 5 and get 10. Subtract $\frac{1}{10}$ of 10, which is 1, and get 9. Add 32 to 9 and get 41.

Answer: 5°C = 41°F

What we just did can be expressed by this formula:

$$F° = \frac{9}{5} \times C° + 32$$

Reference

*Algebra
Word
Problems--
How to
Solve
Algebra
Word
Problems*

*Math Word
Problems*

Here is the formula again. You can use this if you want to go from Celsius to Fahrenheit.

$$F° = \frac{9}{5} \times C° + 32$$

EXAMPLE 2

Problem: Convert 5° Celsius to Fahrenheit.

Solution: Use the formula. We're trying to find F. The C in the formula is 5 for this problem. So we write $F° = \frac{9}{5} \times 5 + 32 = 9 + 32 = 41$.

Answer: 5°C = 41°F

DIRECTIONS

Each number given is a Celsius temperature. Convert it to a Fahrenheit temperature. Use the formula at the top of the page.

PROBLEMS

255. 35°

256. 25°

257. 10°

258. 37° (This answer is not a whole number. Write it as a mixed number.)

Reference

Algebra Word Problems— How to Solve Algebra Word Problems

Math Word Problems

DIRECTIONS

Each number is a Fahrenheit temperature.

Convert it to Celsius. Here is a formula you can use:

$$C° = \frac{5}{9} \times (F° - 32)$$

EXAMPLE

Problem: 86°

Solution: We're trying to find C. For this problem, F = 86. Then the formula says $C° = \frac{5}{9} \times (86 - 32) = \frac{5}{9} \times 54 = 5 \times 6 = 30$.

Answer: 86°F = 30°C

PROBLEMS

259. 41°

260. 68°

261. 32°

262. 212°

263. 104°

Reference

Classroom
Quickies—
Books 1–3

WATER JUGS PROBLEMS

PROBLEM

264. You have three jugs and a well from which to draw water.

The jugs are known to hold exactly 5, 9, and 12 quarts.

Tell how you can use these jugs to measure exactly 7 quarts of water.

Did you know that in many parts of the world, snow is sometimes blue, green, red, or black because microscopic plants are in the air or because dust is collected as the snow falls?

Reference

Classroom Quickies— Books 1–3

REARRANGE LETTERS

DIRECTIONS

Use the letters at the top to fill in the chart so that words are formed and the sentence makes sense.

- A shaded space in the chart shows the end of a word.

- Except for the last line, the end of a line is not the end of a word unless there is a shaded space there.

- When you have filled in the chart, answer the question asked.

PROBLEM

265.

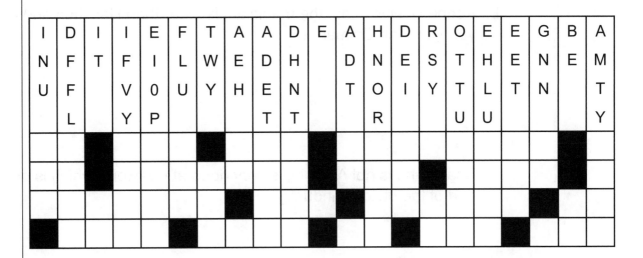

MIND BENDERS®

PROBLEMS

266. Antonia, Colleen, Emmanuel, and Gustave, whose last names are Dewey, Hamilton, Kennedy, and Shaw, are a biologist, a flight attendant, a magician, and a plasterer.

Match up everything from the clues below.

a. The man who is the flight attendant, who is not Kennedy or Dewey, is twenty-five.

b. Kennedy, who is not the magician, is older than Hamilton and is younger than Emmanuel.

c. Shaw, who is not Antonia, is very good at her work, which is not part of the building industry.

d. Antonia is not the plasterer.

Chart for Problem 266

	last name				occupation			
	D	H	K	S	B	FA	M	P
A								
C								
E								
G								
B								
FA								
M								
P								

first name

occupation

Reference

Taken from Mind Benders® B-4

267. Four married couples (Creightons, Farmers, Garsons, Ordways) met in the park for a potluck picnic. They took apple pie, bean salad, iced tea, and potato salad (one item per couple). The husbands' first names are Brad, Edward, Homer, and Ken. The wives' first names are Daphne, Lisa, Moira, and Norma.

Match up everything using the clues below.

a. Brad and his wife, who didn't take iced tea, rode to the picnic with the Ordways, who didn't take apple pie, in their car.

b. Moira and her husband went to the picnic on their motorcycles.

c. The farmers went to the picnic on their bicycles.

d. The Creightons didn't go to the picnic in a car.

e. Homer and Mrs. Farmer went swimming while Mr. Farmer and Edward played horseshoes with Lisa and Daphne.

f. Edward, who didn't go to the picnic in a car, did not take apple pie or bean salad.

g. Brad, who isn't married to Daphne, did not take apple pie or bean salad.

Reference

Taken
from
Mind
Benders®
B-4

Chart for Problem 267

	wife				last name				potluck			
	D	L	M	N	C	F	G	O	AP	ES	IT	PS
B												
E												
H												
K												
C												
F												
G												
O												
AP												
BS												
IT												
PS												

husband

last name

potluck

LIGHT-YEARS

LESSON

Some numbers are so large that they are almost meaningless to us because our minds can't grasp their immensity. For example, how far is 10,000,000,000,000 (ten trillion) miles?

Because of the stupendous distances they deal with, astronomers measure in *light-years* rather than in miles or kilometers.

A light-year is the distance light travels in a year at a speed of 186,282 miles a second.[*]

DIRECTIONS

If you compute with a calculator (or computer), use 186,282 miles a second for the speed of light. If you have to do everything by hand, use 186,000 miles a second. Use 365 days for a year.

PROBLEMS

268. How many seconds are there in

    a. an hour?

    b. a day?

    c. a year?

---

[*]This is the speed light travels in a vacuum. Interstellar space is so empty that any difference between actual speed and speed in vacuum is not considered to be significant.

Reference

Math
Word
Problems

269. How far does light travel in
a. an hour?

b. a day?

c. a year?

270. How far is a light-year?

271. How long would it take a space ship traveling at a million miles an hour to go one light-year?

Reference

*Math
Word
Problems*

272. Alpha Centauri is the star (other than our sun) that is the nearest to Earth.

Actually, Alpha Centauri is a cluster of three stars, named Alpha Centauri A, Alpha Centauri B, and Alpha Centauri C.

Alpha Centauri C revolves around the other two.

Because Alpha Centauri C comes closer to our sun than either of the others, it is also called Proxima Centauri (the nearest star of Centaurus).

Proxima Centauri is about $4\frac{1}{3}$ light-years from us.

a. How many miles away from us is Proxima Centauri?

b. If Proxima Centauri exploded today, how long would it be before people on Earth could know about it?

INDEX OF REFRACTION

LESSON

Light does not travel through a medium (air or water, for instance) at the same speed as it travels in a vacuum.

To find the speed of light in a medium, we divide light's speed in a vacuum by a number called the index of refraction of the medium.

For example, if a medium has an index of refraction of $1\frac{1}{5}$, the speed of light through this medium would be (in miles per second) about $186,000 \div 1\frac{1}{5} = 186,000 \div (6/5) = 186,000 \times \frac{5}{6} = 155,000$.

DIRECTIONS

For this problem, use 186,000 miles a second as the speed of light in a vacuum.

The problem tells you what the medium is and what the index of refraction is. Find the speed of light in that medium.

Give your answer to the nearest whole mile per second.

PROBLEM

273. a. water; index of refraction of $1\frac{3}{10}$

    b. glass; index of refraction of $1\frac{1}{2}$

    c. diamond; index of refraction of $2\frac{2}{5}$

Reference

*Basic
Thinking
Skills*

FOLLOWING DIRECTIONS

DIRECTIONS

Take a sheet of paper and a pencil (or pen).

Each part of the problem tells you to do something. Do it all on the same sheet of paper.

When you are told to suppose something, keep supposing it until the end of the problem.

PROBLEM

274. a. Print your name in the upper-left corner of your paper.

b. Write your teacher's name in the lower-right corner of your paper.

c. Suppose Hussayn is Kasha's older brother. If Kasha was born before Hussayn was born, then draw a rectangle in about the center of your paper. Otherwise, draw a scalene (lopsided) triangle in the upper-right corner of your paper.

d. Put a dot inside the figure you drew for part c.

e. Suppose today is Thursday. If it was Tuesday three days ago, write the name of your street just above your teacher's name. If it will be Saturday three days from now, write the name of your street just below your name.

f. If both "if" parts in the last two sentences of part e are right, write "right" below the figure you drew for part c. If both of those "if" parts are wrong, then write "wrong" above the figure you drew for part c. Otherwise, write the name of your street just before your name.

g. Kasha has a younger sister, Zahra. If Hussayn could be the same age as Zahra, print "same" about halfway between the center of your paper and the bottom edge. If Hussayn has to be older than Zahra, print "older" about halfway between the center of your paper and the top edge. If Hussayn has to be younger than Zahra, print "younger" alongside the figure you drew for part c.

h. Put a dot below the word you printed for part g.

i. Draw a segment whose endpoints are the two dots you made.

Reference

*Basic
Thinking
Skills*

*Mind
Benders®
A-1–A-4*

MIND BENDERS®

PROBLEM

275. Anton, Brigette, and Charles each entered a pet in the school's "Unusual Pets" show.

The pets, which their present owners have had for the past three years, took the three top prizes.

The pets were a gerbil, a turtle, and a white rat.

Use the information below to find each person's pet and the prize it took.

a. This was the first show for Brigette's pet.

b. Anton's pet was not the white rat.

c. Charles's pet won a higher prize than Anton's pet.

d. In last year's show, the turtle won a higher prize than the white rat.

e. Anton's pet won a higher prize than Brigette's pet.

Reference

Math Word Problems

MISCELLANEOUS PROBLEMS

PROBLEM

276. The U.S. Postal Service does not charge a constant rate per ounce on ordinary first-class letters.

Instead, you pay the full rate on the first ounce, but you get to send additional ounces at a cheaper rate.

This cheaper rate continues through about 11 or 12 ounces, and if the package is heavier and you still want it to go first class, you are charged by the pound. This charge varies according to how far you want to send it.

(Free information: When you get charged by the pound, the mail is called "priority" mail instead of "first-class" mail.)

a–c. When first-class postage was 15¢, each additional ounce up through a total of 12 ounces was 13¢. How much was the postage on a first-class letter that weighed

  a. 2 ounces?

  b. 5 ounces?

  c. 12 ounces?

d–f. For first-class postage of 22¢, each additional ounce up through a total of 12 ounces was 17¢. How much was the postage on a first-class letter that weighed

d. 3 ounces?

e. 6 ounces?

f. 12 ounces?

g–i. For first-class postage of 25¢, each additional ounce up through a total of 11 ounces was 20¢. How much was the postage on a first-class letter that weighed

g. 2 ounces?

h. 8 ounces?

i. 12 ounces?

Reference

*Algebra
Word
Problems—
Diophan-
tine
Problems*

*Classroom
Quickies—
Books 1–3*

DIOPHANTINE PROBLEMS

PROBLEM

277. Eunice has won so many of Jonathan's marbles by this time that she's trying to sell some back to him.

The price of marbles has generally gone up since Jonathan bought them the last time, but he has talked Eunice into agreeing to prices of 6¢ each for shooters, 4¢ each for red marbles, and 5 for a penny for multicolored marbles.

How many of each can he get if he buys 100 marbles for $1?

What does "buying a pig in a poke" mean?

Reference

Classroom Quickies— Books 1–3

REARRANGE LETTERS

DIRECTIONS

Use the letters at the top to fill in the chart so that words are formed and the sentence makes sense.

- A shaded space in the chart shows the end of a word.

- Except for the last line, the end of a line is not the end of a word unless there is a shaded space there.

- When you have filled in the chart, answer the question asked.

PROBLEM

278.

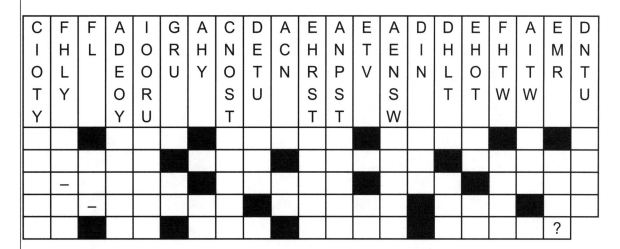

C	F	F	A	I	G	A	C	D	A	E	A	E	A	D	D	E	F	A	E	D
I	H	L	D	O	R	H	N	E	C	H	N	T	E	I	H	H	H	I	M	N
O	L		E	O	U	Y	O	T	N	R	P	V	N	N	L	O	T	T	R	T
T	Y		O	R			S	U		S	S		S		T	T	W	W		U
Y			Y	U			T			T	T		W							

Reference

*Classroom
Quickies—
Books
1–3*

WATER JUGS PROBLEMS

PROBLEM

279. You have three jugs and a well from which to draw water.

The jugs are known to hold exactly 5, 9, and 12 quarts.

Tell how you can use these jugs to measure exactly 13 quarts of water.

A horse's height is measured in "hands." For example, the height of a Clydesdale horse is about 16 to 17 hands, and the height of a Shetland pony is from 8 to 11 hands. How much (what measure) is this kind of hand?

MISCELLANEOUS PROBLEMS

PROBLEM

280. A game was played in which words were to be made from seven given letters.

During one part of the game, double points were given for the first letter of any word formed.

George and Lorna both used all seven letters for their words, but George's word began with *C* (usually 3 points), while Lorna's word began with *E* (usually 1 point).

Whose word was worth more, and how much more? (Or isn't enough information given for you to tell?)

How many feet are in a mile?

MATH MIND BENDERS®

LESSON

Your answers will be numbers. An answer might have one or more digits. Only one digit of an answer goes in a square.

Some of the squares in the grid are numbered so that they may be easily named.

"1-A" means that the answer starts in square 1 and reads across.

"4-D" means that the answer starts in square 4 and reads down.

1-A is a two-digit answer. (In the second grid 1-A is 47.) Two-digit answers also go in 1-D (45), 4-D (12), and 5-A (32).

One-digit answers go in 2-D (7), 3-A (5), 4-A (1), and 5-D (3).

As you can see, this kind of grid will take eight answers.

DIRECTIONS

For each problem, copy the grid here and fill it in.

- You are given some of the answers to a problem. Arrange them so that they all fit into the grid.

- If you are given something like 3 × 4, find the product, which is 12, and fit 12 (not 3 and 4) into the grid.

- There may be more than one way to arrange the answers, but you need to find only one way.

- If the answers you are given will not all fit into the grid, then tell why not.

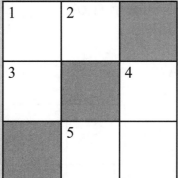

PROBLEMS

281. 9 × 5; 46; 6 × 7; the square of 5

282. For this problem, you are told where one of the answers must go.

3 × 9; 4 × 7; 4-D = 20 + 5 − 7; 3 × 10 − 1

283. 27, 29, 21, 25

Reference

*Math
Mind
Benders®—
Warm-
up and
Warm-
up 2*

LESSON

Here is a sample problem. You will see that a short story is followed by clues that tell you where the answers go. No answer begins with 0.

You will not necessarily be able to fill in the answers in the same order as the clues are given.

SAMPLE PROBLEM

Ramona is 2 years older than Lance, who is 3 years older than Horace. Ramona's great-aunt Martha is a jet pilot.

ACROSS	DOWN
1. Age of Pat, Ramona's brother	1. Ramona's age
3. Test problems Ramona got wrong yesterday	2. Horace's age
4. Lance's age	4. Age of Great-aunt Martha's father
5. 4 × half of 1-A	5. Age of Spot, Ramona's cat

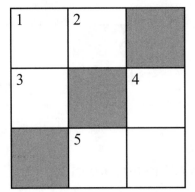

Only clues 4-A, 1-D, and 2-D are connected with the story. Notice that 1-D is a two-digit answer, and 4-A is a one-digit answer.

1-D is 2 more than 4-A (given in the story), so 1-D must be 10 or 11. If 1-D were 10, then 3-A would be 0, which is forbidden. So 1-D is 11, and 4-A is 9. Then 2-D is 6.

Reference

Math Mind Benders®— Warm -up and Warm- up 2

Here is the sample problem again, along with what we have filled in so far.

SAMPLE PROBLEM

Ramona is 2 years older than Lance, who is 3 years older than Horace. Ramona's great-aunt Martha is a jet pilot.

ACROSS	DOWN
1. Age of Pat, Ramona's brother	1. Ramona's age
3. Test problems Ramona got wrong yesterday	2. Horace's age
4. Lance's age	4. Age of Great-aunt Martha's father
5. 4 × half of 1-A	5. Age of Spot, Ramona's cat

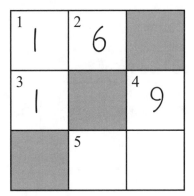

Now go to clue 5-A, which says to take 4 × half of 1-A. Half of 1-A is 8. Then 4 × 8 = 32, so 5-A is 32.

All squares are filled in now. We go back and read the clues we have ignored until now, in order to make sure there are no contradictions. These are clues 1-A, 3-A, 4-D, and 5-D. In each case, the answer is suitable.

Reference

Math Mind Benders®— Warm-up and Warm-up 2

DIRECTIONS

In the clues, "A" means across, and "D" means down. For example, "4-D" would refer to clue number 4 DOWN.

Each square takes a single digit from 0 through 9.

No answer begins with 0.

PROBLEM

284. Emil's age is double Dorothy's and 3 years more than Francine's. Dorothy's great-aunt Martha is a crop duster in Australia.

ACROSS	DOWN
1. Age of Emil's cousin Luke	1. Emil's age
3. Years Luke has been a swim champion	2. Dorothy's age
4. Francine's age	4. Age of Great-aunt Martha with digits reversed
5. 1-D × 2	5. Age of Woofer, Emil's dog

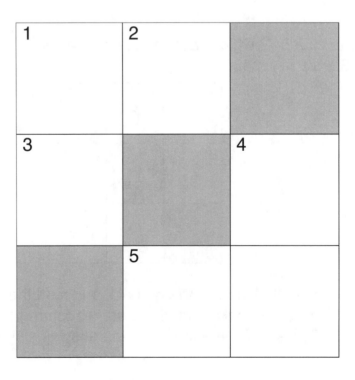

Reference

Math Mind Benders®— Book A-1

DIRECTIONS

In the clues, "A" means across, and "D" means down. For example, "4-D" would refer to clue number 4 DOWN.

Each square takes a single digit from 0 through 9.

No answer begins with 0.

PROBLEM

285. Barney's great-aunt Martha likes to make up puzzles.

She said she'd take him for a ride in her vintage Rolls-Royce if he could solve this puzzle within 10 minutes.

The only thing she would tell him about the puzzle was that she had started out with a certain number.

ACROSS		DOWN	
1.	Great-aunt Martha's age 30 years ago	1.	Cube of 2-D
3.	Barney's age	2.	Great-aunt Martha's starting number
4.	Square of 2-D	4.	See 5-A
5.	4-D ÷ 3-A − 2	5.	Pizzas Barney ate today

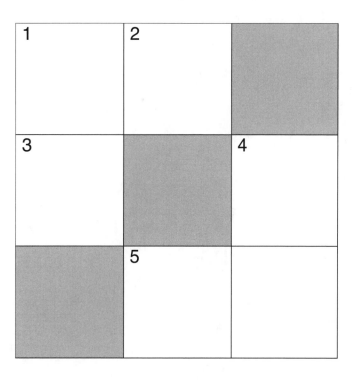

REPLACING LETTERS

PROBLEM

286.

```
    R O S E
  + R E D
  ───────
        2
  S C E N T
```

MISCELLANEOUS PROBLEMS

PROBLEMS

287. A rainfall of 1 inch = a moist snowfall of 6 inches.

a–d. How many inches of rainfall would = a moist snowfall of

a. 9 inches?

b. 4 inches?

c. $1\frac{1}{2}$ feet?

d. 1 foot 3 inches?

e–g. How many inches of moist snowfall would = a rainfall of

e. 3/4 inch?

f. 1/6 foot?

g. 5/6 inch?

Reference

*Math
Word
Problems*

288. If a beat-up catcher's mitt is worth six baseball cards, and if two baseball cards are worth a small bag of marbles, and if a small bag of marbles costs $1, then

   a. how much money is a beat-up catcher's mitt worth?

   b. how much money is a baseball card worth?

   c. how many beat-up catcher's mitts would have the same value as four dozen baseball cards?

   d. how many small bags of marbles would be a fair exchange for a dozen baseball cards?

   e. how many large bags of marbles would be a fair exchange for a dozen baseball cards?

Reference

*Inductive
Thinking
Skills*

NUMBER PATTERNS

DIRECTIONS

For each problem, at least three parts are shown. The next part has a question mark.

Figure out what was done to the first part to get the second part.

See if the same thing was done to the second part to get the third part. (If it wasn't, go back and start again.)

There is a pattern followed to get each change. Find the pattern, and then use it to replace the question mark with the correct numbers.

EXAMPLE

Problem: a. 1   b. 1, 2

c. 1, 2, 3   d. ?

Answer: d. 1, 2, 3, 4

(What was done to part a to get part b? A comma was inserted, and the next number was listed. What was done to part b to get part c? The same thing—a comma, and then the next number. So to get part d, we do the same thing again—insert a comma and list the next number.)

PROBLEMS

289. a. 1   b. 10
c. 100   d. ?

290. a. 1   b. 101
c. 10101   d. ?

Reference

*Inductive
Thinking
Skills*

291. a. 45   b. 56
c. 67   d. ?

292. a. 12   b. 1234
c. 123456   d. ?

293. a. 1, 2   b. 2, 4
c. 4, 8   d. ?

294. a. 1   b. 5
c. 25   d. 125
e. ?

295. a. 123   b. 246
c. 492   d. 984
e. ?

NUMBERED BLANKS

DIRECTIONS

Use letters to fill in the answer blanks by the definitions. Under each of these blanks is a number. Find that number at the bottom of the page and put the letter there, too. When you are through, there will be a question and answer at the bottom of the page.

PROBLEM

296. DEFINITIONS

a. To compute $78 \times 46 - 35$, find a____ ___ then _____

b. $9 \times 10 - 1$

c. Someone who acts silly is told to stop being ____ ____.

d. Ancient Greeks used ____ ____ instead of a hand calculator

e. A person stops being a teenager at the age of ____.

f. 1330_{eleven}

g. What to say when you goof

ANSWERS

$\overline{45}\ \overline{34}\ \overline{8}\ \overline{5}\ \overline{17}\ \overline{18}\ \overline{4}$

$\overline{28}\ \overline{40}\ \overline{22}$

$\overline{44}\ \overline{9}\ \overline{38}\ \overline{12}\ \overline{34}\ \overline{32}\ \overline{18}\ \overline{4}$

$\overline{11}\ \overline{13}\ \overline{10}\ \overline{19}\ \overline{33}\ \overline{15}\ \overline{}$

$\overline{42}\ \overline{47}\ \overline{31}\ \overline{35}$

$\overline{41}\ \overline{14}\ \overline{20}\ \overline{23}\ \overline{46}$

$\overline{43}\ \overline{25}$

$\overline{26}\ \overline{27}\ \overline{37}\ \overline{18}\ \overline{17}\ \overline{44}$

$\overline{12}\ \overline{24}\ \overline{36}\ \overline{29}\ \overline{48}\ \overline{7}$

$\overline{3}\ \overline{39}\ \overline{30}$

$\overline{1}\ \overline{2}\ \overline{6}\ \overline{16}\ \overline{21}\ \overline{44}$

$\overline{1}\ \overline{2}\ \overline{3}\ \overline{4}\quad \overline{5}\ \overline{6}\quad \overline{7}\ \overline{8}\ \overline{9}\quad \overline{10}\ \overline{11}\ \overline{12}\quad \overline{13}\ \overline{14}\quad \overline{15}\ \overline{16}\ \overline{17}$

$\overline{18}\ \overline{19}\ \overline{20}\ \overline{21}\quad \overline{22}\ \overline{23}\ \overline{24}\ \overline{25}\quad \overline{26}\quad \overline{27}\ \overline{28}\ \overline{29}\ \overline{30}\ \overline{31}\ \overline{32}\quad \overline{33}\ \overline{34}\ \overline{35}\ \overline{36}$?

$\overline{37}\quad \overline{38}\ \overline{39}\ \overline{40}\ \overline{41}\ \overline{42}\ \overline{43}\quad \overline{44}\ \overline{45}\ \overline{46}\ \overline{47}\ \overline{48}$

Reference

*Math Word
Problems*

MISCELLANEOUS PROBLEMS

PROBLEM

297. If six children can solve six problems in six minutes,

    a. how many minutes will it take twelve children to solve twelve problems?

    b. how many children will it take to solve twelve problems in twelve minutes?

    c. how many problems can twelve children solve in twelve minutes?

WEIGHING BALLS

PROBLEM

298. You have four balls, all of which look exactly the same.

Three of them all weigh the same, and the fourth one is slightly lighter or heavier.

You have a balance scale. How can you find the odd ball in at most two weighings?

TEACHING SUGGESTIONS AND ANSWERS

INTRODUCTION

Many people assume that the critical thinking needed for mathematics automatically transfers to other subject areas. Research, however, shows that no such transfer generally occurs *unless the student is taught to think critically in a variety of contexts.*

It has also been shown that not only is there no transfer of critical thinking activity outside the subject area but that there is often no transfer *even within the subject area* unless the teacher *teaches for transfer.*

The remedy for this is to involve the student in many facets of critical thinking, both inside and outside a mathematical context, so that (s)he is likely to think critically when confronted with new information.

Consequently, many of the problems in this series do not involve mathematics per se but concentrate rather on developing various aspects of critical thinking needed for success in mathematics. These aspects include the following:

- analyzing a problem to determine a solution (rather than jumping to a conclusion)
- applying old knowledge to new situations
- arriving at a conclusion by process of elimination
- catching contradictions and inconsistencies
- deductive reasoning
- determining whether information is relevant or irrelevant
- distinguishing among possible, probable, and necessary inferences
- inductive reasoning
- learning that there may be various ways to solve a problem
- looking for a logical starting point in a problem that seems unsolvable
- organizing data so that it can be more easily used
- perceiving logical patterns
- using proof by contradiction (indirect proof)
- realizing that a problem may have more than one acceptable solution
- reasoning by analogy
- trying something to see if it works when logic doesn't suggest a solution

- weighing given information to determine truth or falsity

GENERAL INFORMATION

In some subjects, learning need not occur in a particular order. In geography, for example, knowledge about the frequency of earthquakes and other natural phenomena in country X can come before or after knowledge of X's rivers and principal industries, which, in turn, can come before or after any knowledge about country Y.

In arithmetic, however, we have a different situation. Long division comes after subtraction and multiplication, which, in turn, come after addition; division by a two-digit number comes after division by a one-digit number. Nearly every new arithmetic process learned needs application of a previous process learned thereby demanding a review of, and broadening the scope of, prior knowledge.

In recognition of the merit of review, much of the new material introduced at one level in this series is reintroduced at a higher level. With rare exceptions, however, the difficulty of the problems increases as the level increases. The exceptions occur for one of three reasons: (1) The problem has proved to be fun for various ages; (2) A relatively difficult problem is included at a lower level so that the gifted student is challenged; or (3) A relatively easy problem is included at a higher level so that the slower student has success.

Students tend to react negatively to a crowded textbook page and to give it only cursory attention in order to get through it. The result, of course, is that not much critical thinking occurs. On the other hand, the students are suspicious of a comparatively empty page and tend to concentrate on and think about the material there because they intuitively feel that it can't be as easy as it looks.

With this in mind, nearly every page in this series has a generous amount of white space, and the amount of white space on any one page is pretty much in direct proportion to the amount of thought or discussion required to solve the problems on it. In fact, sometimes only one relatively short problem appears on a page, and in these cases intuition is correct: the problem, which may or may not *look* simple, either requires a good deal of thought or has a history of needing much class discussion because different students produce different answers for it.

A few routine problems are included in some sections of this series in order to give the students practice in using a new concept, but the great majority of the problems are designed to stimulate critical thinking. Most of the pages are intended to be used as supplementary materials taking fifteen minutes or so of class time.

Problems range from relatively easy to relatively hard. To judge whether or not you think the problem is appropriate for your class, it is suggested that you do each problem yourself before assigning it.

At the bottoms of some pages are either statements or questions that have no bearing on the other material there. Some are included simply because they are interesting to think about or to know, and others are intended either as nonsense or as mild jokes.

Several of the problems in this series are similar to problems that can be found in recreational mathematics books. Such books usually have a different Dewey decimal number (793) than ordinary books on mathematics (510), but recreational problems can sometimes be found in both of these categories, as well as others. Check with your school and public librarians for their practices in numbering such books.

ARITHMETIC LEVELS OF THIS SERIES

Not all schools are able to teach an optimal arithmetic curriculum. High absenteeism, lack of parental support, and negative peer pressure can combine to frustrate the teachers' attempts to stick to the syllabus. With this in mind, the arithmetic required by the problems in this series has been geared toward the reduced syllabi.

This does not imply that the critical thinking levels of the problems have also been limited. The ages of the intended students have been considered, but otherwise it has been assumed that whatever arithmetic the students know, they are capable of thinking critically about it.

Specifically, the ages and arithmetic knowledge assumed are as follows:

BOOK 1: 8–10 years old, Grades 3–4. The arithmetic assumes only the most basic knowledge of fractions (such as knowing that half of twelve is six) and includes no complicated addition or subtraction, no long multiplication or division, and

no decimals, percents, or areas. Multiplication is usually limited to knowing simple facts such as $3 \times 4 = 12$. Division is similarly restricted.

BOOK 2: 10–12 years old, Grades 5–6. It is assumed that the student can handle integral addition and subtraction, simple long division and multiplication, addition and subtraction of simple mixed numbers, and multiplication and division of simple fractions. With one exception, no three-digit divisors are used. No complicated fractions, percents, or areas are included. Problems involving decimals are limited to students who use hand calculators. These same problems offer alternative numbers to students who must figure by hand.

BOOK 3: 12–14 years old, Grades 7–8. Reasonable facility with the four basic operations using integers or fractions is expected. Decimals rarely appear and then are limited to simple percent or money problems or to students who use hand calculators. A working knowledge (but not a profound understanding) of percents and simple areas is assumed. Some problems involve simple powers.

BOOK 4: age 14 years and older, Grades 9–12. The arithmetic here expects general facility with the four basic operations on integers, fractions, and decimals, along with the ability to work reasonably well with percents and areas. Some problems involve simple powers and simple square roots. No college preparatory mathematics knowledge is expected, but some problems demand fairly complex reasoning about arithmetic.

REFERENCES

At the top left of many pages you will see the word "REFERENCE" followed by one or more titles. These titles correspond to the list below and indicate that similar material can be found in The Critical Thinking Co. publications.

ALGEBRA WORD PROBLEMS
    AGES AND COINS
    DIOPHANTINE PROBLEMS
    FORMULAS, RECTANGLES, D=rt
    FUN TIME
    HOW TO SOLVE ALGEBRA WORD PROBLEMS
    MISCELLANEOUS A-1
    MISCELLANEOUS B-1
    MISCELLANEOUS C-1
    MIXTURES
    PERCENTS AND WORK RATES
    TEACHER'S MANUAL AND DETAILED SOLUTIONS
    WARM-UP

BASIC THINKING SKILLS
CLASSROOM QUICKIES
    BOOK 1
    BOOK 2
    BOOK 3
CRITICAL THINKING, BOOK 1
CRITICAL THINKING, BOOK 2
CROSSNUMBER™ PUZZLES
    SUMS: BOOK A-1
    SUMS: BOOK B-1
    SUMS: BOOK C-1
DEDUCTIVE THINKING SKILLS (MIND BENDERS®)
    MIND BENDERS®—A1
    MIND BENDERS®—A2
    MIND BENDERS®—A3
    MIND BENDERS®—A4
    MIND BENDERS®—B1
    MIND BENDERS®—B2
    MIND BENDERS®—B3
    MIND BENDERS®—B4
    MIND BENDERS®—C1
    MIND BENDERS®—C2
    MIND BENDERS®—C3
    MIND BENDERS®—INSTRUCTIONS AND
DETAILED SOLUTIONS
    MIND BENDERS®—WARM-UP
INDUCTIVE THINKING SKILLS
MATH MIND BENDERS®
    BOOK A-1
    BOOK B-1
    BOOK C-1
    WARM UP
    WARM UP-2
MATH WORD PROBLEMS

TEACHING THINKING

If we are to encourage our students to think critically, we have to give them time to do so, for critical thinking entails more than simply looking at a problem and immediately knowing the answer. With this in mind, avoid doing your students' thinking for them. Encourage them to reason out the answers themselves.

Don't think you have to know all the answers. If you're really teaching your students to think critically, they'll ask many questions you won't be able to answer.

Students are proficient imitators. Show by example the way you want them to react under various conditions:

- Encourage questions, including questions about opinions you've expressed.
- Treat the students courteously and insist they be courteous to each other during a discussion. An argument can be spirited, even heated, without resorting to name-calling or other derogatory comments. Don't allow something like, "That's really a stupid thing to say!" to pass. Insist that the student who says it either apologize or back it up.
- Make learning a team effort, with yourself as part of the team.
- Don't try to fake your way. If you change your mind about an answer, tell the students, particularly if it was their arguments that convinced you. If you don't know an answer, say forthrightly, "I don't know." You might like to add something to that admission: "I wonder how we could find out?" Or, "That's beyond my education." Or, "Let me think about it and see if I can come up with an answer for tomorrow."
- Encourage class discussion, especially of different
  - viewpoints
  - ways of looking at a problem
  - ways of attacking a problem
  - answers to a problem

Some problems might be too hard for an individual student to solve and unsuitable for discussion by the full class. Try grouping the students in sets of three to five to work on these. Decide on the groupings beforehand so that you have at least one good thinker, and preferably two, in each group. Avoid grouping the best and poorest thinkers together. Have the students move their desks so that each group is a self-contained circle.

ANSWERS AND COMMENTS

Page 1
ANSWERS

1. a. Three. When the first marble is chosen, the color doesn't matter. If the second marble matches it, we're done. If it doesn't, then we have two different colors, and the third marble has to be the same color as one of the first two.

   b. Seven. The first six chosen might all be the same color.

I don't know.

Page 2

Because parts a, b, and c of the problem do not appear in the order in which the answers will be found, the problem would be easier if the three parts were eliminated and replaced by the simple question, "Where did each dog hide its bone?" However, it is important for the students to realize that the order in which an author states questions is sometimes arbitrary and that it may be easier to answer a later question first.

It is also possible that an author thought the questions to be stated not arbitrarily but in a logical sequence, each answer helping with the answer to a later question, whereas a student might use a different line of reasoning and find that rearranging the order of the questions makes solving the problem easier.

In either case, the student should be taught to have no compunction about reading through all questions to be answered and choosing to start with whichever one seems the easiest.

ANSWERS

2. The bulldog's bone is not near a hedge or a tree (both given), so it is by a fence. Then the fox terrier's bone is not the one by a fence, nor is it near a tree (given), so it is under a hedge. This leaves the boxer's bone to be the one behind a tree.
   a. fox terrier
   b. boxer
   c. bulldog

Page 3

ANSWER

3.

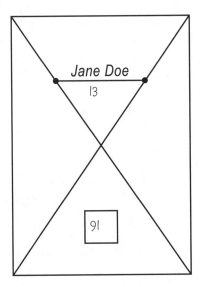

Pages 4–6

ANSWERS

4. Stephen, Randall, Inez
5. Not enough information
6. in front of the house with the red roof
7. a mile
8. Tasha, Jacob, Erica
9. Yes. Maybe Ludwig was absent today.
10. 30¢
11. Not enough information

Pages 7–15

Students too often make unwarranted assumptions about what they're reading or being told. A painless way to show them that they do this is to supply them with a short story and some conclusions about a subject that is simple to understand, emotionally neutral, and interesting enough to argue about. Fairy tales and nursery rhymes not only meet these criteria but have the added advantage of being so familiar that the students are doubly likely to allow past impressions of the story to influence their interpretations of what they are now reading.

Use class discussion to decide on the answers. For each answer, ask first, "How many chose 'true'? How many 'false'? How many 'can't tell'?" and write the numbers on the chalkboard. Ask, "Who wants to start? Tell us which answer you chose and why you think it's right." Try to keep out of the discussion yourself. Let the students argue about it until they are all convinced of the same answer. It will take longer to settle without your intervention, but it will be more effective in developing the students' abilities to think critically.

Don't take for granted that my answers have to be right. I once used the same problem for three different classes, went to the first class knowing my answer was right, changed my mind because of the students' arguments, and changed my mind twice more because of the arguments of the students in the other two classes.

Don't think your students are too old for nursery rhymes and fairy tales. My students were tenth- through twelfth-graders whose abilities ranged from gifted to educable mentally retarded and whose social inclinations ranged from aggressive gang members to shy loners. Despite the ages of the students and the numerous classes exposed to such materials, there were only a handful of times when a student objected to the first problem with a disparaging, "Hey, we're a little old for this kind of stuff, aren't we?" In each case, I said to the class after obviously considering the student's comment, "You could be right at that. I'll tell you what. I'll make a deal with you. If you'll all read the story to yourselves and decide on the first five answers without talking to anyone about them, and if we all agree on the answers, we won't do any more of the problem, and we'll move on to something else." The students thought this fair enough and set to work. It sometimes took two class periods (55 minutes each) to agree on the first answer, and that was the end of any objections.

ANSWERS

12. a. T
b. T
c. ?
d. T
e. T
f. T
g. ?
h. ?
i. F. She may or may not have been clumsy, but she didn't have to be.
j. ?. The frog said the sorcerer was wicked, but that doesn't mean it's true.

13. a. ?
b. ?
c. T
d. F
e. ?
f. ?
g. F. We must accept the story as true, and the story said it was made of gingerbread.
h. F
i. T
j. ?
k. T
l. T
m. F
n. ?
o. ?
p. T
q. ?
r. ?
s. T. This is implied by the word "that." If "that" were changed to "if" or "whether," then this answer would be "?."
t. ?
u. F

v. ?
14. a. T
b. ?
c. ?
d. ?
e. F
f. T
g. F
h. T
i. ?
j. ?
k. ?
l. ?
m. ?
n. T
o. T
p. ?
q. F. We are instructed to accept the story as true, so we cannot admit the possibility that the story lied to us.

Pages 16–20

These problems teach the students that the easiest place to start on a problem is not necessarily at the first number one encounters. They also teach that one may have to consider and discard various choices before finding one that satisfies all conditions.

Although it may look as though there could be more than one answer, these problems are created so that the answers are unique.

For those teachers who haven't encountered this type of problem before, a detailed solution is given to the first problem.

ANSWERS

15. Start with 16. This can't be 7 + 9 (because 0 can't be used in the sum for 10). So 16 = 9 + 7, and 15 = 9 + 6. Now 10 is not 7 + 1 + 2 (because 17 can't be 6 + 1 + 10), so 10 is 7 + 2 + 1, which makes 17 = 6 + 2 + 9 and forces the other answers.

16.

Kakuro grid with clues and entries: 16, 12; 14, 9; 11, 10; 21, 9 1 7 4, 4; 5, 2 3, 3/17, 2 1; 14, 2 8 1 3; 13, 4 9

17.

Kakuro grid with clues and entries: 16, 15; 9, 7 2; 3, 10; 15, 1 2 9 3, 7; 5, 2 3, 11/17, 6 5; 15, 1 8 4 2; 13, 4 9

Pages 21–39, 53–56

One of the most important mathematical tools is the ability to recognize and use analogies. When we show our students how to solve a few problems, we want them to apply analogous reasoning to other problems. When we introduce new material, we want them to recognize the similarities and respect the differences between these new ideas and what they already know.

Analogues abound in mathematics. For example, multiplication and addition are analogous, as are division and subtraction. Telling the time seventeen hours after twelve o'clock (using a twelve-hour clock) is analogous to finding the least residue of 17 (mod 12). Arithmetic operations in base ten are analogous to those in base sixteen. A problem asking how many nickels are in $5.25 is analogous to one asking how much would have to be invested at 5% in order to earn $5.25 interest.

Problems involving percents are readily translatable to problems involving fractions or decimals. And if you'll excuse the pun, the reasoning needed to prove plane geometry theorems often runs parallel to that needed for proving theorems in analytic geometry.

If we are to have students who easily recognize analogous situations in mathematics, it is necessary that they learn to look for similarities and differences, that they learn that order matters, that they learn to distinguish between situations that are close enough to be analogous and situations that are not, and that they have practice in forming analogies.

This could be accomplished utilizing only mathematical notions, but it is much easier for the students to learn when the practice exercises use everyday words not taken exclusively from any one subject area. (Presenting an assortment of topics also has the advantage of showing that analogies can be applied in numerous contexts.) Consequently, most of the material on the next few pages has little to do with mathematics per se, but it has a great deal to do with building knowledge necessary to success in mathematics.

After the word "analogous" is introduced in the textbook, it will be assumed throughout the rest of the book that the students will understand an instruction such as, "Use analogous reasoning to show...."

Pages 21–23

ANSWERS

18. floor
19. basement
20. late
21. fiction
22. myth
23. crawl
24. hovel
25. tightwad
26. far
27. open
28. nasty
29. left
30. wrong
31. sharp
32. engrossing
33. sad
34. engrossing

Pages 24–26

You may need to point out that two words may be related by degree and yet have quite different meanings. For example, a laugh and a smile can both indicate pleasure, but they do not mean almost the same thing.

ANSWERS

35. peaceful
36. windless
37. mesh
38. catch
39. profit
40. rotten
41. bird
42. peel
43. reduce
44. kind of fruit
45. set of two
46. sighted
47. vista
48. penny
49. dispatched
50. odor
51. judgment

Page 27

Encourage alternate answers to these problems. We want the students to learn to notice various similarities among apparently different things, for such discernment is a prerequisite to the successful use of analogical reasoning in mathematics.

ANSWERS

52. end
53. ahead of
54. copies
55. liquid measures
56. large residences
57. hat styles

Page 28

ANSWERS

Other answers are not only possible but likely. Encourage class discussion of answers.

58. by design; accidental
59. recently made or harvested; well-preserved
60. bold in a mildly offensive way; insulting
61. briskly attentive; cautious
62. up-to-date; popular
63. large residences; cottage

Pages 29–30

ANSWERS

Other answers are possible.

64. width
65. exit
66. whimper
67. lively
68. learn
69. 6
70. taste
71. physician

Pages 31–32

ANSWERS

72. sum, difference
73. more, plus
74. fact, fiction
75. gentleman, lady
76. week, 7 days
77. good, evil
78. correct, incorrect
79. give, take

Pages 33–35

ANSWERS

80. bake, cake / permit, order / aged, youthful / before, now / sturdy, frail
81. plus, times / plus, minus / subtract, difference / subtract, reduce / deduct, decrease

Pages 36–39

We are reasoning by analogy any time we use a previous experience to predict the outcome of a new experience. For example, "That plant had green leaves, and I was told to pull it out because it was a weed. This plant has green leaves, so it must be a weed, too." Or, "I got yelled at yesterday because I was running in the school hallway. If I run in the school hallway today, I'll get yelled at today, too."

Make sure the students understand that when reasoning by analogy assumes a cause-and-effect relationship, it is the quality of the relationship that determines whether or not the analogy is a good one. In the first example above, the speaker assumes that having green leaves causes a plant to be classified as a weed. Since having green leaves has no bearing on whether or not a plant is called a weed, the analogy is a poor one. In the second example above, it is assumed that running in the school hallway causes the runner to be reprimanded. On the surface, this assumption is false, and yet the analogy is a good one because running in the hallway can be dangerous and it is this potential danger, rather than the running itself, that results in the reprimand.

The students will automatically look for similarities between analogous situations, but you may have to lead them to evaluate the relative importance of the points of agreement.

All analogous situations have differences, too, and some students are likely to say that a particular analogy is poor because differences outnumber similarities. Consequently, you may have to stress to the students that when they are deciding on the quality of an analogy, they are to distinguish between important and unimportant differences.

Here are some other examples of reasoning by analogy.

- That steel bar is metal, and my fingernail doesn't make a dent in it. Since this aluminum foil is also metal, my fingernail won't make a dent in it, either. (Poor.)
- My house is at sea level, and I got scalded when some boiling water splashed on my wrist. I'm now near a campfire on top of a mountain 15,000 feet high, and my wrist will get scalded if boiling water splashes on it. (Poor. Water boils at a much lower temperature at high altitudes outdoors.)
- My friend went to a beauty parlor for a facial, and when they were done she didn't have any wrinkles. So if I go to that beauty parlor and have the same operator give me a facial, then I won't have any wrinkles. (Not enough information. How old is my friend? How old am I? Did my friend have any wrinkles before the treatment? Do I have any wrinkles?)
- Three different batteries for my toy lasted only a month each. So if I get another of the same kind of battery and use the toy the same amount of time, the new battery will last only a month. (Good.)

Use class discussion for these problems. We want the students to be exposed to the reasoning of their classmates and to hear the arguments they use.

ANSWERS

82. I'm undecided about this answer, but I lean toward "just okay." I had a terrible time with decimals in the sixth grade but eventually learned to work with them and never had such

trouble with later arithmetic lessons, so my experience tells me that Henry's conclusion is unjustified. Henry's conclusion does have some justification, however, since Bethany is smarter than he and she's still having trouble.

I could be convinced to choose "need more information" for this one, because there are too many unknown factors. Did either Henry or Bethany ask for help from the teachers or from other people? Did the teachers do a good job of explaining why certain things are done when working with fractions? Did Henry or Bethany spend any extra time trying to understand fractions? Because of the way the brain works, people of equal intelligence don't have equal abilities in all directions, so Bethany's being smarter than Henry doesn't imply that Henry's arithmetic ability is not greater than Bethany's. Is Bethany's arithmetic ability below average? Is Henry's arithmetic ability below par for his age so that he doesn't understand now but will within a year or so?

83. Poor. The color of a cat doesn't cause sneezing. Notice that Janine apparently does not connect her sneezing with petting cats in general but with petting yellow cats.

84. Poor. Baseball bats are made to stand solid hits, so that wasn't what caused Antonio's bat to crack.

Page 40

Puzzles like this provide excellent opportunities for the students to exercise their critical thinking abilities. There are several discoveries for them to make, among which are the following:

(1) When only one letter appears, it can be filled in.

(2) When a word contains only one letter, that letter is *a* or *i* (A single letter could also be an initial—e.g., Harry S. Truman—but not in these particular puzzles.)

(3) To make the remaining choices more obvious, used letters should be crossed off.

(4) Only certain letters can be used to begin or end a two-letter word. For example, no two-letter word begins with *c* or *r* so if the letters *c, r* and *t* are in a column where a two-letter word begins, then *t* is the choice to make. The only ordinary two-letter words starting with *t* are to and *tv*, so any other letters appearing in the next column can usually be ruled out.

(5) A three-letter word starting with *th* is *the* or *thy*.

(6) A three-letter word starting with *y* is probably *yes, yet* or *you*. A three-letter word ending with *u* is probably *you*.

(7) A four-letter word starting with *th* is probably *that, than, them, then,* or *they*

(8) Only certain sequences of letters are probable. For example, words don't begin or end with *rw* or *pm* (but they might begin with *wr* or end with *mp*).

ANSWER

85. I counted from two through a thousand by twos. How many numbers did I count? (500)

Page 41

This is strictly a class discussion problem. If you think, as I did, that this problem's answer is so obvious that your students will be insulted by being given the problem, you have a surprise coming. I've found that the usual answers are gains of 0, $10, $20, or $30, with an occasional answer of a loss of $10, $20, or $30.

Ask the students to call out their answers, and write all the answers on the chalkboard. Then ask, "Who wants to start? Tell us which answer you got, and tell us how you got it." The hard part for the students comes when you say, after hearing the explanation, "We have some other answers here, and we can't have more than one right answer to the problem, so if you think another answer is right, you should be able to tell us what's wrong with the reasoning we've just heard."

The time needed for the discussion usually takes at least a full class period. I've never told my students the answer to the problem. Instead, they have always managed to prove which answer is correct.

ANSWER

86. Not given. Let the students battle it out.

Page 42

ANSWER

87. Take the goose across. Return and take the fox across. Return with the goose and take the corn across. Return and take the goose across.

(a dirty double-crosser)

Page 43

This is a typical Diophantine problem. If we try to solve this problem by straight algebra, we'll have three variables but only two equations—a setup that has an infinite number of solutions. However, a Diophantine problem has built-in conditions that limit the number of solutions. For example, Jonathan can't buy a fraction of a red marble or a negative number of shooters.

The mathematics needed for a *formal* solution of a Diophantine problem is beyond the knowledge of an elementary school student, but the students nevertheless enjoy trying to solve the problems.

A side benefit of presenting the students with Diophantine problems is that the students learn that not all problems are as straightforward as they sound and that such problems can be solved by trial and error.

There are three more Diophantine problems in this textbook.

For information about how to solve Diophantine problems (which may be helpful to you but not to your arithmetic students), as well as for more Diophantine problems to give your students, see the booklet *Diophantine Problems* in the ALGEBRA WORD PROBLEMS series.

ANSWER

88. He can buy 5 shooters, 20 red, and 75 multicolored, or 12 shooters, 8 red, and 80 multicolored.

(to hold up his trousers)

Pages 44–45

Your students should deduce from the last example (no bulldog is green) and from the last paragraph on the page that a statement might be proved false in several ways, of which finding a counterexample is just one. (Working on the principle that there will be at least one student who hasn't made the inference, however, you'd better mention it to the class.)

ANSWERS

89. a. Yes
   b. No. It doesn't disagree with the statement.
   c–d. No. No specific example is given.
   e. No. It doesn't disagree with the statement.
   f. Yes
   g. No. No specific example is given.

Pages 47–50

ANSWERS

90. a. Yes
   b. No
   c. Yes
   d. Yes
   e. No
   f. No
   g. Yes

91. a. Yes
   b. No. No example is given.
   c. No. The statement is based on what would happen if kids did not fool around, not on what happens when they do, so the example does not disagree with the statement.

92. This is not the kind of statement that can have a counterexample.

93. a. No. First, the "and so..." doesn't follow from the first part of the sentence, because there are still games she can play. Second, even if the "and so..." did follow, the fact that she can't play games doesn't imply that she doesn't like to play games.
   b. Not enough information is given here. Does the boy dislike playing games (in which case this is a counterexample), or does he like them well enough but simply prefers to spend his time doing things he likes even better (in which case this is not a counterexample)?
   c. No. The statement makes a claim only about children.
   d. Yes

94. This is not the kind of statement that can have a counterexample.

95. a. No. Although this objection is true, it not only doesn't give a counterexample but also avoids the question of whether or not the given statement is true.
   b. Yes
   c. No. This is similar to the statement in part a.
   d. No. To say someone "doesn't mind" doing something is not to say that he likes doing it. (I don't mind going to the dentist to have my teeth cleaned and checked twice a year, but that doesn't imply that I like doing it.) The speaker also plays baseball in the rain but gives no indication of whether or not (s)he likes it.

Pages 51–52

Although the general rule in this textbook is to include only as much on one page as the students should be expected to learn or solve in one session, these two pages of problems do not follow that rule. There are several items on each page, and it would probably be a good idea to attempt to answer no more than half of the problems on a page in one session.

ANSWERS

96. No. A counterexample is an example that proves a (general) statement to be false, so there can be no counterexample to a true statement.

97. For this problem, encourage the students to think of a set of two statements to use as a model. That is, the two given statements are in the form, "All [word or phrase #1] are [word or phrase #2]. I found a [#1] that is not a [#2]." The questions become less abstract if the students substitute meaningful words or phrases for #1 and #2. Their chosen first statement should be true for some, but not all, cases.
   a. Yes
   b. Yes
   c. No. All zoffers except the one you found may be middigs.
   d. Yes
   e. Same as (c).
   f. Yes
   g. No
   h. No
   i. No. You've proved that a zoffer doesn't have to be a middig, but not the converse. For example, put zoffers = numbers that can be written as fractions, and put middigs = numbers that can be written as whole numbers. Then the statement reads, "All numbers that can be written as fractions are numbers that can be written as whole numbers." The statement can be disproved by producing the fraction 2/3, but that doesn't prove that some whole numbers cannot be written as fractions.

98. For this problem, too, encourage the students to think of a set of statements to use as a model. It will be helpful if the statement is itself true but has a false converse.

a. No. Consider the statement "All squares are four-sided figures." Finding a 3 × 6 rectangle is not a counterexample to the statement.
b. No
c. No
d. No
e. No
f. No
g. No
h. No
i. No
j. Yes

Pages 53–56

Many standardized tests measure knowledge by including analogies among the test questions. However, a wrong answer there may not indicate lack of knowledge about the subject matter. Instead, it may show confusion about what is being asked. This is because in everyday life we don't necessarily compare or contrast two pairs of things by using the standard analogical words "is to" and "as," and these words don't make a lot of sense in such a context unless either we think about them and figure out how they're being used, or we've seen them used previously in such a way and now understand how they relate the terms to each other.

As you discuss this section with your class, keep in mind that an analogy using "is to" and "and" will not, to many of the students, immediately make sense. To help them understand, choose a simple analogy and try stating it in various ways.

Ignoring whether or not good English is used, or even whether or not the statements are entirely accurate, here are some examples of other ways to state the analogy, "Up is to down as high is to low":

- Up and down are related in the same way that high and low are related.
- Up is related to down the way high is related to low.
- Up and down contrast in the way that high and low contrast.
- Up is different from down in the way that high is different from low.
- The relation between up and down is like the relation between high and low.

Similar examples can be formulated using such terms as these: dissimilar, opposite, opposed (to), reversed (from), contrary (to).

So that the students don't get the idea that the first two terms of an analogy must name opposites,

you will probably want to show that analogies can be formed for other relationships, too. At the same time you give a nonstandard form, be sure also to state the standard form, as shown below.

- A cow and its calf are related in the way that a mare and its foal are related. (A cow is to its calf as a mare is to its foal.)
- Laugh and happy sound go together just like cry and sad sound go together. (Laugh is to happy sound as cry is to sad sound.)
- Green light means "go" just as red light means "stop." (Green light is to "go" as red light is to "stop.")

Stress two things: (1) An analogy must always make good sense, and (2) An analogy cannot necessarily be formed from two pairs of terms even if the terms of one pair are related not only to each other but to the terms of the other pair. For example, a hammer and a wrench are both tools, and both are owned by humans; a dog and a cat are both pets, and both are owned by humans. Despite these similarities, however, it wouldn't make good sense to say any of these (or any of the 20 other statements that could be made from arranging the four terms in different orders):

Hammer is to wrench as dog is to cat.
Hammer is to wrench as cat is to dog.
Hammer is to dog as wrench is to cat.
Hammer is to cat as wrench is to dog.

Ask the students to think of analogies themselves (using "is to" and "as"), and let the class discuss whether or not the analogies created are good ones. This not only will supply examples on the students' level but will also lessen confusion about the meaning of an analogy stated in standard form.

ANSWERS

99. Man is to woman as male is to female.
100. Mayor is to city as governor is to state.
101. Fact is to fiction as history is to myth.
102. Snow is to ski as water is to swim.
103. Master is to slave as ruler is to subject.
104. Hammer is to saw as hit is to cut.

Pages 55–56

In the "don't be fooled" paragraph on page 55, the second sentence is accurate only if the four given terms are different from each other. If two of the terms are the same, there will be only twelve distinct ways to arrange them, of which just four will be in correct order for forming analogies. For example, given the terms

ocean, lake, lake, puddle

they can be arranged as

ocean, lake, lake, puddle
ocean, lake, puddle, lake
ocean, puddle, lake, lake
lake, ocean, lake, puddle
lake, ocean, puddle, lake
lake, lake, ocean, puddle
lake, lake, puddle, ocean
lake, puddle, ocean, lake
lake, puddle, lake, ocean
puddle, ocean, lake, lake
puddle, lake, ocean, lake
puddle, lake, lake, ocean

The only acceptable analogies would be
Ocean is to lake as lake is to puddle.
Lake is to ocean as puddle is to lake.
Lake is to puddle as ocean is to lake.
Puddle is to lake as lake is to ocean.

ANSWERS

To avoid having to list eight answers for each problem, a general solution is given here, and then only a first answer is given for each problem.

General rule:

	term	is to	term	as	term	is to	term
If	first		second		third		fourth
then	first		third		second		fourth
and	second		first		fourth		third
and	second		fourth		first		third
and	third		first		fourth		second
and	third		fourth		first		second
and	fourth		second		third		first
and	fourth		third		second		first

105. pencil pen lead ink
106. grass lawn flower garden
107. fan heater cool warm
108. No valid analogy can be drawn.
109. sight sound eyes ears

Pages 57–58

These problems will be too obscure for some of the students to figure out by themselves, and yet to invite a full class discussion could easily lead to so many suggestions and comments that confusion, rather than solution, results. Instead, break up the class into several small groups, say

three to five students each, and let each group work independently on solving the problem.

ANSWERS

110. 1/3 of a (fenced lawn) = 1/3 of a yard = *foot*
(paper and pencil game for two) with no ([clock sound] or [sharp object]) = ticktacktoe with no (tick or tack) = *toe*
penmanship without writing = handwriting without writing = *hand*
(fish structure) followed by (sound of cross dog) = (fin) followed by (grrr) = *finger*
Result: Foot is to toe as hand is to finger.

111. roller coaster with no (hair curler) = roller coaster with no roller = *coaster*
window pane = *glass*
place (tahhsittocS) = place (backward Scottish hat) = place (backward tam) = *place mat*
(LP) without tr = (record) without tr = platter – tr = *plate*
Result: Coaster is to glass as place mat is to plate.

Pages 59–69

Many of us are used to calling a mathematical function, say addition, an "operation," and this terminology is correct. However, a function is an operator as well as an operation. The symbol used to denote the function, say +, is also an operator.

As a point of interest, computer programming manuals consistently refer to mathematical functions as "operators" rather than "operations," and their symbols used as operators include not only +, −, * (multiplication), and / (division) but grouping characters such as ( ) and (( )), logical operators such as "not", "and" and "or," and conditional operators such as < and <=.

Rather than call, say addition, an operation and call its symbol, +, an operator, it is consistent with modern usage and less confusing to the students to say "operator" for both the operation and its symbol.

The order of precedence stated in the textbook is followed both in mathematics and in computer programming.

Only the operators ( ), ×, ÷, /, +, and − are discussed. The addition and subtraction needed are relatively simple, and the multiplication (and allied division) does not go higher than 10×10. More operators are discussed in Books 3 and 4, and the computations there are correspondingly more complex.

Pages 59–63

Stress the importance of working from left to right. Although it doesn't matter for addition and multiplication because they are associative, subtraction and division are not associative, and most students won't stop and think about this if they feel like starting at some point other than the left end. As examples, $24/4/2 = (24/4)/2 \neq 24/(4/2)$, and $10 - 5 - 4 = (10 - 5) - 4 \neq 10 - (5 - 4)$.

Insist that the students show their work so that you can verify their reasoning.

ANSWERS

Answers will vary.

112. $2 \times 3 - 6 = 6 - 6 = 0$
113. $6 - 2 - 3 = 4 - 3 = 1$
114. $6/3 \times 2 = 2 \times 2 = 4$
115. $6 + 2 - 3 = 8 - 3 = 5$
116. $6 \div 2 + 3 = 4 + 3 = 6$
117. $6 + 3 - 2 = 9 - 2 = 7$
118. $6/2 \times 3 = 3 \times 3 = 9$
119. $2 + 3 + 6 = 5 + 6 = 11$
120. $6 + 2 \times 3 = 6 + 6 = 12$

Pages 64–65

You will want to be able to follow the students' reasoning, so make sure they show their work, as in the examples in the lesson and the answers below.

ANSWERS

121. $4 \times 3 \div 2 = 12 \div 2 = 6$
122. $7 - 2 \times 3 = 7 - 6 = 1$
123. $1 + 8 - 3 \times 2 = 1 + 8 - 6 = 9 - 6 = 3$
124. $1 + (8 - 3) \times 2 = 1 + 5 \times 2 = 1 + 10 = 11$
125. $(1 + 8 - 3) \div 2 = (9 - 3) \div 2 = 6 \div 2 = 3$
126. $(8 - 3 \times 2) + 11 = (8 - 6) + 11 = 2 + 11 = 13$
127. $4 \times 6/(3 + 25 \div 5) = 4 \times 6/(3 + 5) = 4 \times 6/8 = 24/8 = 3$
128. $2 \times (24 - 3 \times 3 + 7 - 2 \times 9) = 2 \times (24 - 9 + 7 - 18) = 2 \times (15 + 7 - 18) = 2 \times (22 - 18) = 2 \times 4 = 8$
129. $14 - (2 \times 8 + 2) \div (63 \div 7) = 14 - (16 + 2) \div (63 \div 7) = 14 - 18 \div 9 = 14 - 2 = 12$
130. $57 - (3 \times 7 - 15) \times (5 + 12 \div 4) = 57 - (21 - 15) \times (5 + 12 \div 4) = 57 - 6 \times (5 + 12 \div 4) = 57 - 6 \times (5 + 3) = 57 - 6 \times 8 = 57 - 48 = 9$
131. $72 \div (14 - 24 \div 4) \times (16 - 11) - 4 \times 5 = 72 \div (14 - 6) \times (16 - 11) - 4 \times 5 = 72 \div 8 \times (16 - 11) - 4 \times 5 = 72 \div 8 \times 5 - 4 \times 5 = 9 \times 5 - 4 \times 5 = 45 - 20 = 25$

Pages 66–67

Make sure the students show their work step by step, as in the answers below.

ANSWERS

132. $(2 + 4)/2 = 6/2 = 3$
133. $18 - (6 + 12/3) = 18 - (6 + 4) = 18 - 10 = 8$
134. $(13 + 5)/2 \times 7 = 18/2 \times 7 = 9 \times 7 = 63$
135. $2 \times 6 - (1 + 8) = 2 \times 6 - 9 = 12 - 9 = 3$
136. $7 \times 8 - 5 \times 10 = 56 - 50 = 6$
137. $24/(6/2) + 3 = 24/3 + 3 = 8 + 3 = 11$
138. $14 \div (1 + 6) \times 8 - 1 = 14 \div 7 \times 8 - 1 = 2 \times 8 - 1 = 16 - 1 = 15$
139. $48 \div (12 - 4) \times (14 - 5) = 48 \div 8 \times (14 - 5) = 48 \div 8 \times 9 = 6 \times 9 = 54$
140. $(4 + 2) \times 7 - 9 \times 4 = 6 \times 7 - 9 \times 4 = 42 - 9 \times 4 = 42 - 36 = 6$
141. $(2 + 3) \times 6 - (3 \times 7 + 1) = 5 \times 6 - (3 \times 7 + 1) = 5 \times 6 - (21 + 1) = 30 - 22 = 8$
142. $4 \times (12/2 + 1) + 2 - 5 \times 6 = 4 \times (6 + 1) + 2 - 5 \times 6 = 4 \times 7 + 2 - 5 \times 6 = 28 + 2 - 5 \times 6 = 28 + 2 - 30 = 30 - 30 = 0$

Pages 68–69

These problems provide an admirable way to meet several teaching goals:

- Students do drill work but feel as though they're taking a break.
- The problems are open-ended in two ways: first, there is no guarantee of a solution for any given problem; second, there may be many solutions to a given problem.
- The problems require creative thinking, for there are numerous possible combinations that can be tried (most of which won't work) in order to get an answer.
- The problems demand critical thinking because each time a combination is tried, it must be analyzed and either accepted or rejected. If it is rejected, the student then must try to figure out what is wrong with it and what needs to be changed in order to make the result acceptable.
- The problems provide a gentle way for the students to learn that (1) not all arithmetic problems have solutions, and (2) for some problems that have solutions, these solutions may have to be found by trial and error and a process of elimination.
- Even though finding a particular answer may take

several minutes, the students do not react to their temporary lack of success with a loss of self-confidence, for they understand what is to be done, and they know how to go about doing it.

- The problems present an agreeable challenge. Students enjoy trying to find answers and are likely to spend some of their free time trying to do the problems.

If your students like competition, you could issue a challenge to see who can come up with the greatest number of correct answers for a given problem; for example, $6 = (3 \times 4) \div (1 \times 2) = (4 \times 3) \div (1 \times 2) = ... = 1 + 3 + 4 - 2 = 3 + 1 + 4 - 2 = ... = 12/4 + 3 = $ other combinations, too. Or the challenge could be to see who can find solutions for the longest list of numbers. If you decide on this one, it would probably be a good idea to set an upper limit, say 50 or 100. Otherwise, you're likely to be faced with computations such as 32×41.

ANSWERS

143. There are many ways to get answers. A quick run-through found solutions for all but five of the whole numbers from 0 through 100. I did not find solutions for 53, 74, 89, 95, or 99. Of the ninety-six solutions found, seven used one or both of decimals and square roots, and two used summation signs ($\sum$). There may, of course, be simpler solutions for those I solved, as well as solutions for the five problems I didn't solve.

144. As in the preceding set of problems, there are many correct answers. A quick run-through for this current set found solutions for all whole numbers from 0 through 100. No summation signs ($\sum$) were used this time. It was not necessary to use either decimals or square roots for the first fifty problems, but I used one or both of these in at least twenty-five of the last fifty-one problems. There may, of course, be simpler solutions for several of the problems in the last half.

Pages 70–72

ANSWERS

145. Maybe Lucretia's bus had to make more stops.
146. 2,000 yards
147. a. Betty, Arthur, Mortimer
     b. Mortimer, Arthur, Betty
148. Not enough information

149. Luke and Joan are both in the field of law, so they are not brother and sister. Then Joan is Mark's sister, and Helen is Luke's sister.
150. 32
151. Yes
152. No
153. Not enough information

Page 73

Finding patterns is an important aspect of mathematical development. Most answers will probably agree with the simple patterns shown in the answers below. However, students are used to having only one correct solution to a problem and may assume that an answer must be wrong if it doesn't agree with everyone else's answer, so do encourage those who found different patterns to tell the others about them. This will not only reassure such students but will also demonstrate to the rest of the class that there can, indeed, be more than one logical answer to some kinds of problems.

Also, there can be more than one correct explanation for a given answer, and the students should be asked for their lines of reasoning. For example, when I wrote problem 2, I was thinking of "add 3, subtract 1," but it would be just as logical to think of the pattern as "list the odd numbers, and in between them insert the even numbers, starting with 4."

ANSWERS

154. 9, 10, 12, 13 (Pattern: add 2, add 1.)
155. 8, 7, 10, 9 (Pattern: add 3, subtract 1.)
156. 30, 31, 62, 63 (Pattern: double, add 1.)
157. 16, 22, 29, 37 (Pattern: add 1, add 2, add 3, and so on.)
158. 39, 40, 120, 121 (Pattern: multiply by 3, add 1.)

Pages 74–75

ANSWERS

159. Germaine is not the dentist (given), so Samisoni is the dentist. He is not the electrician or the carpenter (both given), so he is the house cleaner. Then Germaine is the carpenter and the electrician.
160. If the first native told the truth, then the second native lied. If the first native lied, then the second native told the truth. Either way, one of them told the truth and the other lied, so the third native has to be a liar.

Pages 76–80

How often have we seen outlandish answers to mathematical problems? For example, a student gets an answer of 45 to the problem 45 × 9 because "Everyone knows that 0 is nothing, so 45 is the same as 405." (Yet the same student will readily agree that $405 is not at all the same as $45.) Or a student adds three numbers, each of which is between 10 and 20, and is not at all disturbed when his or her answer is not between 30 and 60. It sometimes seems as though such students suspect that mathematics has something to do with magic, in which case, they reason, one answer should be as good as another.

There are various degrees of likelihood to be considered when choosing whether or not to accept something. Among these are the following: fact, highly probable, more likely than not, fifty-fifty, possible but not probable, possible but unlikely, and impossible. Wishful thinking and fantasy probably come somewhere between the last two.

It is important that students learn to think about given information and to distinguish among the various degrees of likelihood. As a first step toward this goal, the two problems following are designed to press the student to make a relatively easy decision about likelihood. Each case is a matter of deciding simply whether a story falls within the bounds of reasonable possibility or whether it falls so far outside these bounds that it becomes mere wishful thinking or fantasy.

ANSWERS

161. a. True to life
   b. Fantasy. (The principal has no such authority.)
   c. Fantasy
   d. Fantasy
   e. Fantasy
   f. Fantasy
   g. True to life
162. a. True to life
   b. True to life
   c. Fantasy
   d. Fantasy
   e. True to life
   f. Fantasy
   g. Fantasy. (It is important that the students acknowledge the fantasy in this story, for it appears to summarize the wishful

thinking of some of them. It is true that an arithmetic lesson may be understood when a previous one was not, but in such a case one of two things will be true, both of which were denied in the story: either the new lesson will clear up the confusion about the previous lesson, or the new lesson will not be based on knowledge taught by the previous lesson.)

Pages 81–82

Make sure the students understand these simple ideas. We're going to use them on clocks other than 12-hour clocks and then expand the ideas to include counting in number bases other than base ten.

ANSWERS

163. 5 o'clock
164. 12 o'clock
165. 2 o'clock
166. 3 o'clock
167. 4 o'clock
168. 9 o'clock
169. 4 o'clock
170. 5 o'clock

Pages 84–86

ANSWERS

171. 2 o'clock
172. 8 o'clock
173. 6 o'clock
174. 6 o'clock
175. 3 o'clock
176. 5 o'clock
177. 6 o'clock
178. 4 o'clock
179. 5 o'clock
180. 2 o'clock
181. 1 o'clock
182. 5 o'clock
183. 3 o'clock
184. 2 o'clock
185. 3 o'clock
186. 8 o'clock
187. 1 o'clock
188. 6 o'clock

Pages 87–88

189. Make sure the students understand exactly how Mario does the problems. His method is much easier than counting out the hours one by one on the fingers. Also, it will help avoid mistakes because some students, when asked for the time 5 hours after 10 o'clock (on a 12-hour clock) will start with 10 and count 10 (one), 11 (two), 12 (three), 1 (four), 2 (five), getting an answer of 2 o'clock.

Left to devise their own arithmetic notation for, say a 12-hour clock, the students are likely to write something like "9 + 7 = 16 − 12 = 4." Do not allow such an incorrect use of "=." Offer an acceptable alternative such as 9 + 7 = 16; 16 − 12 = 4.

ANSWERS

189. a. Yes. When going forward, the clock counts 1, 2, ..., 6 and then starts at 1 again, in effect discarding the first 6 numbers, and that's what Mario's method does. When going backward, the clock counts 6, 5, ..., 1, and then starts at 6 again, in effect adding 6 each time the next number would be less than 1. Again, that's what Mario's method does.

b. 1) He would use 9's instead of 6's.
2) Yes. The principle is the same as explained in (a) above for the 6-hour clock.

c. Same as (b) 2 above.

190. a. Yes. We already know that Mario's method always works. The only difference between his method and Choon-Wei's is that Mario does the problem while working with a large number to be added or subtracted, afterwards reducing the answer by multiples of 6, while Choon-Wei reduces the large numbers to be added or subtracted before doing the problem. The two methods give identical results.

b. She would find 15 − 7 − 7 = 1 and add that to 2, getting an answer of 3 o'clock.

c. Yes. Mario's method works for all clocks and, as explained in (a) above, Choon-Wei's method gives the same results.

Pages 89–90

Encourage the students to try several examples in order to convince themselves that they can use exactly the same computations with this clock that they used for a 6-hour clock whose numbers were 1–6, except that whenever they would have had an answer of 6, they will now have an answer of

0. Make sure they understand that this applies only to a final answer—i.e., that they still have to add or subtract multiples of 6, not 0, when doing their computations. For example, 19 hours after 2 o'clock, it will be 2 + 19 − 6 − 6 − 6 = 3 o'clock.

ANSWERS

191. 2 o'clock
192. 4 o'clock
193. 0 o'clock
194. 5 o'clock
195. 4 o'clock
196. 0 o'clock
197. 2 o'clock

Pages 91–97

Students tend to be confused when, after having been carefully taught to distinguish between numerals and numbers, they read a sentence such as, "What are the factors of 12?" It's obvious to them that 12 is a numeral, and a numeral is just something made from a given set of symbols, so how can a numeral have factors? Or are the factors the symbols that make up the numeral, so that the factors of 12 are 1 and 2?

A different, but related, question is raised in the students' minds when they read, "What are the factors of the number 12?" because now they read that the symbol "12" is no longer a numeral but has suddenly become a number, which they know is not possible. So perhaps the question should be, "What are the factors of the number represented by the numeral 12?" That seems to be a complicated way to ask what should be a simple question.

The textbook avoids such difficulties by using the word "number" when referring either to a numeral or to a number. This is correct usage according to the dictionary, and the students are not confused, for they judge by context (as they do for so many other words).

Pages 91–93

The concepts here are so well known that the students may tend to skim through the lesson, thinking the material is too elementary for them. To know something and to understand it thoroughly, however, are two different things, and what we want is for the students to understand these ideas so well that they will be able to apply analogous reasoning to number bases other than base ten.

ANSWERS

198. $38 = 3 \times 10 + 8 \times 1$
199. $70 = 7 \times 10 + 0 \times 1$
200. $99 = 9 \times 10 + 9 \times 1$
201. $506 = 5 \times (10 \times 10) + 0 \times 10 + 6 \times 1$
202. $480 = 4 \times (10 \times 10) + 8 \times 10 + 0 \times 1$
203. $217 = 2 \times (10 \times 10) + 1 \times 10 + 7 \times 1$
204. $3145 = 3 \times (10 \times 10 \times 10) + 1 \times (10 \times 10) + 4 \times 10 + 5 \times 1$

Pages 94–95

The value of our written numbers depends on both the base used and the place a digit occupies. The definition of a "base n number system" includes the stipulation of place value for each digit.

Our way of writing numbers is sometimes called a "base and place number system." Not all number systems use the concept of base and place. For example, Roman numerals (how many digits are there?) do not have a place value. "XI" = 11, and "XC" = 90, showing that "X" takes a value of 10 one time and a value of −10 another time, even though it is in the same place both times.

ANSWERS

205. 1, 2, 3, 4, 10, 11, 12, 13, 14, 20, 21, 22, 23, 24, 30, 31
206. 1, 2, 3, 4, 5, 10, 11, 12, 13, 14, 15, 20, 21, 22, 23, 24, 25, 30, 31
207. 1, 2, 3, 4, 5, 6, 10, 11, 12, 13, 14, 15, 16, 20, 21, 22, 23, 24, 25, 26, 30, 31
208. 1, 2, 3, 4, 5, 6, 7, 10, 11, 12, 13, 14, 15, 16, 17, 20, 21, 22, 23, 24, 25, 26, 27, 30, 31
209. a. The difference would be 8. If we did convert the two numbers to base ten, we'd have 8 × 96 and 8 × 97, a difference of 8. Encourage the students to realize this without actually doing the multiplication and subtraction involved. There are at least three ways they could think of this:
1) Regardless of how much 97 × 8 and 96 × 8 are, 97 8s is one more 8 than 96 8s.
2) Think of 97 and 96 8s to be added:
97 of these: 8 + 8 + 8 + ... + 8 + 8
96 of these: 8 + 8 + 8 + ... + 8
Now when we subtract one list from the other, all 8s except the last one in the 97 string will be eliminated.
3) If your students are familiar with the

distributive property, use it here: 8 × 97 − 8 × 96 = 8 × (97 − 96) = 8 × 1 = 8.
b. Same answer. The last digit doesn't matter because it is a units digit (i.e., × 1) for all three bases and so will be eliminated when finding the difference between the two numbers.

Page 96

ANSWERS

	base five	base ten
210.	21	$2 \times 5 + 1 \times 1 = 10 + 1 = 11$
211.	44	$4 \times 5 + 4 \times 1 = 20 + 4 = 24$
212.	132	$1 \times (5 \times 5) + 3 \times 5 + 2 \times 1 = 25 + 15 + 2 = 42$
213.	420	$4 \times (5 \times 5) + 2 \times 5 + 0 \times 1 = 4 \times 25 + 10 + 0 = 100 + 10 + 0 = 110$
214.	1000	$1 \times (5 \times 5 \times 5) + 0 \times (5 \times 5) + 0 \times 5 + 0 \times 1 = 125 + 0 + 0 + 0 = 125$
215.	1020	$1 \times (5 \times 5 \times 5) + 0 \times (5 \times 5) + 2 \times 5 + 0 \times 1 = 125 + 0 + 10 + 0 = 135$

Page 97

ANSWER

216. We are going to add in base five exactly as we do in base ten, except that we remember to regroup by fives instead of by tens. For example, here are two base five problems:

```
  31        24
+ 12      + 34
  43       113
```

(The computations in this explanation are in base ten.) The first problem looks the same in both base five and base ten. For the second problem, 4 + 4 = 8 = 5 + 3, so we enter 3 and carry a five to the fives column. Then 1 + 2 + 3 = 6 = 5 + 1, so that's 5 fives + 1 five. We enter 1 in the fives column and carry 1 five × five to the next column. This second computation becomes clearer when we remember that $5_{ten} = 10_{five}$. This makes $8_{ten} = 5_{ten} + 3_{ten} = 10_{five} + 3_{five} = 13_{five}$, so we enter 3 and carry 1 to the fives column. In the fives column, $1 + 2 + 3 = 6_{ten} = 5_{ten} + 1_{ten} = 10_{five} + 1_{five} = 11_{five}$, so we enter 1 in the fives column and carry 1 to the five × fives column.

Page 98

This is another Diophantine problem.

ANSWER

217. Of shooters, red marbles, and multicolored marbles, respectively, he can buy 12, 4, and 84; or 8, 11, and 81; or 4, 18, and 78; or 0, 25, and 75.

Who knows? Roosters don't lay eggs.

Pages 99–103

ANSWERS

218. What is the sum of four and two thirds and one and three fourths? ($6\frac{5}{10}$)

219. Fill the 11-liter jug from the river. Fill the 7-liter jug from the 11-liter jug and the 5-liter jug from the 7-liter jug. This leaves 4 liters in the 11-liter jug and 2 liters in the 7-liter jug. Empty the 5-liter jug.

I don't know.

220. The key to the solution lies in realizing that all three pens are now mislabeled. It doesn't matter which pen Jody starts with. Suppose he chooses the one labeled "black," and Nina says it is the blue pen. This leaves the red and black pens to identify. One is labeled "red," and the other is labeled "blue." The red pen isn't labeled "red," so it is the one labeled "blue." Then the black pen is the remaining pen, the one labeled "red."

221. 280¢ or $2.80

222. a. 50¢
b. 10¢

223. Put one ball in each pan. If the scale doesn't balance, you've found the odd ball. If the scale does balance, remove the two balls weighed and weigh two others. If the scale balances, the odd ball is the one still unweighed. If the scale doesn't balance, you've found the odd ball.

Page 104

The students may not realize at first that they have worked with proportions many times before, and it would be helpful to remind them that every time they have added or subtracted fractions with unlike denominators, they have written at least one proportion. For example, given the fractions 2/3 and 5/6 to add, they have written "2/3 = 4/6" and probably also "5/6 = 5/6."

It is important that the students have clear ideas about the parts of a proportion, their relation to each other, the significance of the equal sign, and the difference between a ratio and a proportion.

Stress that "equal" is a symmetric relation, so this is always true: If item 1 = item 2, then item 2 = item 1.

All fractions are ratios. Although there are various kinds of ratios, all ratios in this book are fractions, so for the most part the two words can be used synonymously by the students.

There is a difference in the thinking involved about the two concepts, however: a fraction, say 3/4, is thought of as 3 parts out of every 4 parts (of something), whereas the ratio 3/4 is thought of as 3 to 4 because a ratio compares the two things.

For example, in a household comprised of a baby, two parents, and a grandparent, 3 out of 4, or 3/4, of the people are adults, and the ratio of adults to total people is 3 to 4, or $\frac{3}{4}$.

A ratio has two terms: $\frac{\text{first term}}{\text{second term}}$ or $\frac{\text{numerator}}{\text{denominator}}$

A proportion has two sides, left-hand side = right-hand side, or first ratio = second ratio, and four terms: $\frac{\text{first term}}{\text{second term}} = \frac{\text{third term}}{\text{fourth term}}$.

A proportion is read this way: first term is to second term as third term is to fourth term.

As defined here, a proportion consists of two ratios separated by an equal sign, so for our purposes neither of the following is a proportion:

- 4/2 = 2 [but 4/2 = 2/1 is a proportion]
- 4/2 = 24/3 – 6 [but 4/2 = (24 – 18)/3 is a proportion, as is 4/2 = 24/(3 + 9)]

In common usage, the terms "ratio" and "proportion" are sometimes used interchangeably. In mathematics, however, the two terms are never synonymous. Here are some of the differences:

- A proportion is a statement of equality, a ratio is not.
- A proportion contains an equal sign, a ratio does not.
- A ratio gives the relative sizes of two things, a proportion is a statement that two pairs of things have the same relative sizes.
- A ratio is not in itself a statement, a proportion is.
- A proportion has four terms, a ratio has only two.
- A proportion is an equation, a ratio is not.

Pages 105–6

It is not suggested that you raise the matter

yourself, but some of the students may conjecture, since any proportion can be written as an analogy, that any numeric analogy can be written as a proportion. If they do bring it up, encourage them to explore the idea. They should be able to think of various counterexamples to the conjecture. For instance, if we're talking about differences between numbers, then

1 is to 2 as 5 is to 6, but $1/2 \neq 5/6$.

Or if we're talking about multiplying a number by itself, then

9 is to 3 as 25 is to 5, but $9/3 \neq 25/5$.

In each of these cases, however, no pair of numbers was a ratio, for a ratio, by definition, is a fraction—i.e., an indicated *quotient* of two numbers—and this should be made clear to the students. In the first case above, for instance, to talk about the *difference* between 1 and 2 and then to write "1/2" is contradictory. Although nonproportional numeric analogies can be formed, nonproportional numeric analogies cannot be formed when the numbers compared are ratios.

ANSWERS

All of the proportions are listed here, although the students are required to state only three of them. However, only the first of the analogies are shown here. In particular, notice that we consider the proportion $a/b = c/d$ to be distinct from the proportion $c/d = a/b$, even though they are equivalent statements.

224. Yes. $1/5 = 2/10$; 1 is to 5 as 2 is to 10; $1/2 = 5/10$; $5/1 = 10/2$; $5/10 = 1/2$; $2/10 = 1/5$; $2/1 = 10/5$; $5/1 = 10/2$; $5/10 = 1/2$.

225. No

226. Yes. $2/4 = 1/2$; 2 is to 4 as 1 is to 2; $2/1 = 4/2$; $4/2 = 2/1$; $1/2 = 2/4$. Notice there are only four distinct proportions here.

227. Yes. $1/8 = 3/24$; 1 is to 8 as 3 is to 24; $1/3 = 8/24$; $8/1 = 24/3$; $8/24 = 1/3$; $3/24 = 1/8$; $3/1 = 24/8$; $24/3 = 8/1$; $24/8 = 3/1$.

228. Yes. $2/9 = 4/18$; 2 is to 9 as 4 is to 18; $2/4 = 9/18$; $9/2 = 18/4$; $9/18 = 2/4$; $4/18 = 2/9$; $4/2 = 18/9$; $18/4 = 9/2$; $18/9 = 4/2$.

229. No

230. Yes. $3/4 = 6/8$; 3 is to 4 as 6 is to 8; $3/6 = 4/8$; $4/3 = 8/6$; $4/8 = 3/6$; $6/8 = 3/4$; $6/3 = 8/4$; $8/6 = 4/3$; $8/4 = 6/3$.

231. Yes. $10/15 = 8/12$; 10 is to 15 as 8 is to 12; $10/8 = 15/12$; $15/10 = 12/8$; $15/12 = 10/8$; $8/12 = 10/15$; $8/10 = 12/15$; $12/8 = 15/10$; $12/15 = 8/10$.

Pages 107–22

The students at this level are not asked for proofs. Rather, they are encouraged to explain their findings informally by being asked, "How come?" or by being told to "tell" or "explain" why something is true or false. The answers given here are sometimes correspondingly informal, although most of the answers also include proofs in case they are needed.

The problems are arranged in their approximate order of difficulty. Although they look innocuous enough, these problems require critical thinking and will result in a decidedly improved understanding of ratios and proportions.

Furthermore, finding the answer to such a problem is one thing, but proving it is considerably more difficult.

The students may need frequent reminders to choose numbers of their own so that they can see how a problem works. Encourage them to start each problem with easy numbers. For example, if a problem says that two terms of the proportion are the same, they could start with $1/2 = 2/4$ or $2/4 = 4/8$; if the terms are all distinct, they could start with $1/2 = 3/6$ or $2/4 = 3/6$. Once they see how the problem works for these numbers, they can try to generalize their findings so that specific numbers don't have to be used. This generalization is, of course, the hard part of the problem and requires a different level of critical thinking (and a different side of the brain) than merely understanding the problem and trying it out with specific numbers.

Use class discussion to help the students graduate from an intuitive understanding to the formulation of a proof that their intuition is correct. It will be helpful if you will

a. remind them that if both numerator and denominator of a fraction are multiplied or divided by the same (nonzero) number, the fraction's value doesn't change (Mention again that they've done such multiplication and division when adding or subtracting fractions with unlike denominators.)

b. remind them that dividing a fraction by a number is the same as multiplying the fraction by the number's reciprocal

c. teach them that both sides of an equation can be multiplied or divided by the same (nonzero) number, and the result will also be an equation

d. Show them several examples of a–c and assign a few problems for practice, possibly along these lines:

(1) Change each fraction into a fraction having a denominator of 12: 1/2, 2/3, 5/6

(2) Find a common denominator for each pair of fractions and express both as fractions having that denominator: 2/3, 3/4; 1/2, 3/7; 2/5, 3/20

   (Notice that the least common denominator [LCD] is not asked for. Encourage the students to realize that a pair of fractions can have an infinite number of common denominators.)

(3) Find the LCD for each pair of fractions, and express both as fractions having that denominator: 6/12, 6/8; 6/16, 2/4; 8/24, 4/6

(4) Reduce each fraction as far as possible: 4/6, 10/20, 15/25

(5) Multiply both terms by 2, 3, and 5: 1/2, 3/5, 2/6

(6) Multiply both sides by 3: 1/2 = 3/6; 8/5 = 16/10

(7) Divide both sides by 2: 2/1 = 6/3; 8/9 = 24/27

Even when they can prove something orally you should not expect students at this level to be able to prove it in *writing*, at least not with a conventional proof. Instead, you might like to encourage them to use diagrams (with numbered or lettered parts, if they wish) and arrows to go along with a written explanation.

You will notice that on some pages a list of selected problems proved so far is included. This helps the students remember some properties of proportions and serves as a handy reference if needed for the current problem. It is also a sneaky way to let the students know that not everything included on a page is needed for the problem they're doing.

Some of the last problems here are rather difficult for this level, but they were included in order to stretch the critical thinking ability of the average student (even though the student does not solve the problem completely) and to challenge the gifted student. It is suggested you try a problem yourself before assigning it to your class.

Pages 108–9

ANSWERS

232. The remaining number must be the same as the other three. Two of the three equal numbers must be the terms of one of the ratios, so that ratio is worth 1. Then the other ratio, too, must be worth 1, and so its two terms have to be equal.

233. You can always switch the sides of an equation. (Formal reason: By definition, the equals relation is symmetric.)

234. Different examples may be given for the "yes" answers.
   a. Yes. 1/2 = 2/4
   b. Yes. 1/2 = 3/6
   c. Yes. 2/4 = 3/6

Page 110

The students aren't asked to produce examples, but they will probably do so in order to convince others that their answers are right.

ANSWER

235. Although the students are not asked at this point to prove anything, there are six possible exchanges: terms 1 and 2, 1 and 3, 1 and 4, 2 and 3, 2 and 4, 3 and 4. Of these, only two will always work: terms 1 and 4, and 2 and 3. The other exchanges will never work (under the given conditions—i.e., with four distinct positive terms). Problem 245 asks for proof that there is always at least one arrangement that won't work.

Pages 111–12

ANSWERS

236. a. Three answers are possible—40, 5/8, and 8/5—but only 40 is expected at this stage.
   b. Using 40 as the fourth number, two proportions are 1/5 = 8/40 and 1/8 = 5/40. (Note: A later problem asks that all three possible answers be found.)

237. a. 4; 2/2 = 3/3
   b. 4; 1/2 = 2/4
   c. 8; 1/2 = 3/6

Page 113

This theorem will be used in later proofs, so it would be a good idea to stress it and make sure the students understand it and can say it. The correct statement of the theorem includes the stipulation in part a that the numerators are nonzero, but that was omitted here because the initial conditions stated for these problems in the students' text excluded zero as one of the terms of a proportion.

ANSWER

238. The students' explanations may be something like this:

A proportion says the two ratios are equal. You can't have something like 2/3 = 2/5 or something like 2/4 = 3/4 because they aren't equal, and the same thing would be true no matter what numbers you used.

A more formal proof would increase the difficulty level of the problem, but here is such a proof:

a. Divide both sides of the equation by a numerator. Then multiply both sides by the product of the denominators. Reduce the results as far as possible. The end result says the denominators are equal.

b. Multiply both sides by a denominator and reduce the results as far as possible. The end result says the numerators are equal.

Page 114
ANSWER

239. If the other ratio's terms were equal, then that ratio would be worth 1. But the ratio with the unequal terms wouldn't be worth 1, and so the two ratios wouldn't be equal. Then they couldn't be proportional, which contradicts what we're given.

Page 115
This theorem will be used in later proofs.
ANSWER

240. Use the product of the denominators as a common denominator, and convert the two ratios to ratios having this denominator. The denominators are now equal, so the numerators are equal (problem 238), and the problem is proved. (The left-hand numerator is the product of the extremes, and the right-hand numerator is the product of the means.)

Page 116
Don't let your students reason that this problem can be proved by using problem 240 as evidence, for problem 240 is the converse of this one, and converses are not always true. For example, if something is a cat, then it is an animal; but it is not true that if something is an animal, then it is a cat.

This is not an especially hard problem for this level, once the students start thinking seriously about how to apply the hint given, and it is suggested that you don't give any hints about

how to apply the hint. However, you might like to give them several examples (similar to the one in their text) to make sure they understand what the problem is claiming.

The problem doesn't ask for proof that either pair of the given numbers can be chosen as the extremes or that this pair and the means pair can be used in either order or that any of the four given numbers can be used as the first term of the proportion. The students are quite likely to take for granted that these things are true, and it is probably a good idea at this level to let them make use of the concepts without pointing out to them that they are using unproved ideas.

This theorem will be used in later proofs.
ANSWER

241. We're given an equation having (a product of) two numbers on each side. Choose a number from the left-hand side, and divide both sides of the equation by this number. Reduce the left-hand side so that this number is eliminated. Do the same thing for a number from the right-hand side (choose, divide, reduce). The result is a proportion in which the given left-hand pair are the extremes, and the given right-hand pair are the means.

Pages 117–19
ANSWERS

242. Use problem 240 to get the product of one pair of numbers = the product of another pair of numbers. Then use problem 241 to arrange
a. the means, and
b. the extremes
in the other order

243. Yes. Use problem 240 (product of the extremes = product of the means). Then using problem 241, choose the two numbers on the right-hand side (the old means) to be the extremes of a new proportion. Choose the old second term as the new first term, and choose the old first term as the new second term.

244. The students may come up with different answers for the different parts of the problem, but all answers can be the same: A proportion can be formed, so problem 240 guarantees that our four given numbers can be paired in such a way that the product of one pair = the product of the other pair. Choose a number for the first term of the proportion. Then (problem 241) the other number in that pair will be the fourth term, and the remaining two numbers will be the second and third terms (in either order).

Page 120

It is not enough to show an example here, for that would show only one case for which the statement was true, whereas what is needed is a proof that the statement is always true.

ANSWER

245. The numbers are distinct, so there is a largest number and a smallest number. Use the largest number as the first term and the smallest number as the second term of the proportion. Then the quotient of these two numbers has to be larger than the quotient of the remaining two numbers because these latter two numbers are closer together in size. Since the quotients are unequal, the ratios that indicate them are unequal, so the ratios are not proportional.
(Note: This was touched on in problem 235, although at that point proof was not asked for.)

Page 121

ANSWERS

246. a. Only 3, which are 5/8, 8/5, and 40.
b. 8

Page 122

This is estimated to be one of the harder problems, not because the proof is demanding, but because students at this level have difficulty realizing that if one number divides another, then all factors of the first number are also factors of the second.

ANSWER

247. Multiply both sides of the equation by the left-hand ratio's denominator, leaving a whole number on the left. Then the right-hand ratio's denominator has to divide into the new right-hand numerator a whole number of times (in order to have a whole number on the right, too). Therefore, each factor of the right-hand denominator is also a factor either of the original left-hand denominator or of the original right-hand numerator.

Pages 123–24

ANSWERS

248. What is the answer to twelve divided by three fourths? (16)

249. Fill the 5- and 7-gallon jugs and empty them both into the 11-gallon jug, leaving 1 gallon in one of them. Empty the 11-gallon jug. Dump the 1 gallon into it. Fill the 7-gallon jug.

> None. The rest of them ran away, too.

Page 125

This is another Diophantine problem.

ANSWER

250. Of shooters, red marbles, and multicolored marbles, respectively, he can buy 2, 30, and 68; or 5, 25, and 70; or 8, 20, and 72; or 11, 15, and 74; or 14, 10, and 76; or 17, 5, and 78; or 20, 0, and 80.

> a pride of lions

Page 126

ANSWERS

251. a. 48
b. 146
c. 51
d. 81
e. 40
f. 55

Pages 127–34

Many students seem to take for granted that almost anything said during a discussion has a bearing on the topic. They assume that if a comment touches on a peripheral issue, then it is germane to the subject at hand. This is evidenced by their thinking, say, that an assignment to write a theme on "Why I Like Dogs" is satisfied by a theme on "Why I Like Dogs Better Than Cats."

The ability to differentiate between relevant and irrelevant thoughts is vital to critical thinking in mathematics. When we are doing a three-column addition problem, for instance, it doesn't do much good to think about how multiplication of fractions is done, but it does help to think about how a two-column addition problem is done and to apply the same principles here.

Use class discussion for these problems. Although the directions don't ask for reasons for the answers, ask the students why they chose their answers. Their reasons will help clarify the difference between relevant and irrelevant comments both for themselves and their classmates.

ANSWERS

252. a. Yes
b. Yes
c. No
d. No. (She could go to college to get the education needed.)
e. Yes
f. Yes
g. Yes
h. No
i. Yes
j. Yes
k. No
l. No
m. Yes
n. No
o. No
p. Yes. (As it stands, the statement is relevant. Whether or not age has anything to do with being a good teacher is a different question.)

253. a. Yes
b. No
c. No
d. Yes
e. Yes
f. No
g. Yes
h. No
i. No
j. Yes, if she's concerned only about doing the homework even though she might not get credit for it from her teacher. No, if she wants credit for doing it and the teacher wouldn't give it to her.

254. a. Yes
b. No
c. No
d. Yes
e. No
f. Yes
g. Yes
h. No
i. No

Pages 135–43

ANSWERS

255. 95°
256. 77°
257. 50°
258. $98\frac{3}{5}°$ (Written in its more usual form, this is 98.6°, the normal body temperature.)
259. 5°
260. 20°
261. 0°
262. 100°
263. 40°
264. Fill the 12-quart jug from the well. Fill the 9-quart jug from the 12-quart jug, and fill the 5-quart jug from the 9-quart jug. Empty the 5-quart jug.
265. If you add thirteen and fifteen and then multiply the result by five, what do you get? (140, we hope)
266. Parenthesized letters refer to clue letters in the problem.
Shaw, a female (c), is not Antonia (c), so she is Colleen. Emmanuel is not Kennedy or Hamilton (b), so he is Dewey.
The flight attendant, a male (a), isn't Emmanuel Dewey (a), so he is Gustave. His last name is not Kennedy (a), so it is Hamilton, and so Antonia is Kennedy. The plasterer is not Shaw (c) or Kennedy (d, Antonia), so he is Dewey. Kennedy is not the magician (b), so Shaw is and Kennedy is the biologist.
    Antonia Kennedy, biologist
    Colleen Shaw, magician
    Emmanuel Dewey, plasterer
    Gustave Hamilton, flight attendant
267. Parenthesized letters refer to clue letters in the problem.
    Mr. Farmer, who went on a bicycle (c), is not Brad (a, car) or Homer or Edward (e), so he is Ken. Mrs. Farmer, who also went on a bicycle (c), is not Moira (b, motorcycle) or Lisa or Daphne (e), so she is Norma.
    Brad, who went in a car (a), is not married to Moira (b, motorcycle) or Daphne (g), so he is married to Lisa. Then Brad and Lisa are not the Creightons (d, no car) or the Ordways (a), so they are the Garsons.
    Ordway went in a car (a), but Edward didn't (f), so Edward isn't Ordway. Then Homer

is Ordway, and Edward is Creighton. The Farmers went on bicycles (c), the Garsons (Brad and wife) and the Ordways went in a car (a), and the other couple, who are the Creightons, went on motorcycles (b). Then Edward Creighton is married to Moira (b), and Homer Ordway is married to Daphne.

The apple pie was not taken by the Ordways (a), the Creightons (f, Edward), or the Garsons (g, Brad), so the Farmers took it. Brad didn't take iced tea (a) or bean salad (g), so he took potato salad. Edward didn't take the bean salad (f), so Homer took it, and Edward took the iced tea.

   Brad and Lisa Garson, potato salad
   Edward and Moira Creighton, iced tea
   Homer and Daphne Ordway, bean salad
   Ken and Norma Farmer, apple pie

Pages 144–46

Stress to the students that a light-year is a measure of distance, not a measure of time. Once they have grasped this concept, questions about time (e.g., "How long does it take for light to reach Earth from Proxima Centauri?") may confuse them, and it may take several examples of analogous problems to clarify the situation.

   Suggested examples include the following:

- You want to go 100 miles (distance). How long will it take (time) if you go at 50 mph (rate)?
- A racehorse ran at an average speed of 30 mph (rate). How long did it take (time) for the horse to go around a 1-mile track (distance)?
- Your friend's house is 264 feet away (distance). If you run all the way at 15 mph (rate), how many seconds (time) will it take you to get there?
- The sun is 93,000,000 miles away (distance). Light travels at 186,000 miles a second (rate). How long does it take the sun's light to reach us?
- Proxima Centauri is 4 3/10 light-years away (distance). Light travels at 186,282 miles a second (rate). How long does it take light from Proxima Centauri to reach Earth?

Encourage the students to use hand calculators for these problems. They will have to use their critical thinking abilities to figure out how to get the calculator to do the required work when the numbers to be entered or the answers are beyond the calculator's capacity. (If the problem requires

division, and if the divisor has more digits—not counting trailing zeros—than the calculator's capacity, allow the divisor to be rounded off.)

ANSWERS

First answers are for 186,000 and 365; second answers are for 186,282 and 365.

268. a. 3,600
    b. 86,400
    c. 31,536,000
269. a. 669,600,000 miles; 670,615,200
    b. 16,070,400,000 miles; 16,094,764,800
    c. 5,865,696,000,000 miles; 5,874,589,152,000
270. 5,865,696,000,000 miles; 5,874,589,152,000 miles
271. There are 24 × 365 = 8,760 hours in a year, so the space ship would travel 8,760,000,000 miles in that time. Then the answers are (hand) 5,865,696,000,000 ÷ 8,760,000,000 = 669 3/5 years; (calculator) 5,874,589,152,000 ÷ 8,760,000,000 = 670.6152 ≈ 670 3/5 years.
272. a. 25,418,016,000,000; 25,456,552,992,000
    b. about $4\frac{1}{3}$ years

Pages 147–48

ANSWERS

273. a. 143,077 miles a second
    b. 124,000 miles a second
    c. 77,500 miles a second

274.

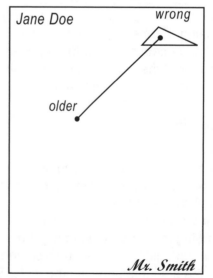

Page 149

ANSWER

275. Notice that the given information rules out the possibility of any switching of pets since last year's show. Combining items (a) and (d), Brigette's pet is the gerbil. This, with item (b), makes Anton's pet the turtle and leaves the white rat as Charles's pet. Items (c) and (e) give us the prizes won.

<u>Summary</u>

first prize, Charles's pet, white rat
second prize, Anton's pet, turtle
third prize, Brigette's pet, gerbil

Pages 150–51

ANSWERS

276. a. 28¢
    b. 67¢
    c. 158¢ or $1.58
    d. 56¢
    e. 107¢ or $1.07
    f. 209¢ or $2.09
    g. 45¢
    h. 165¢ or $1.65
    i. Not enough information is given to answer this. (Actually, it went into the priority mail rates, and the cost was $2.40.)

Page 152

This is another Diophantine problem.

ANSWER

277. He can get 2 shooters, 18 red marbles, and 80 multicolored marbles.

> It means buying something without seeing what you're getting. Farmers sometimes used to take a pig to market tied in a poke (a bag or sack), so whoever bought the pig without untying the poke and looking inside was buying a pig in a poke.

Pages 153–55

ANSWERS

278. If you started with a dollar and spent thirty-four cents and then twenty-eight cents, how much do you have left? (38¢)

279. Fill the 12-quart jug from the well. Fill the 9-quart jug from the 12-quart jug. Empty the 9-quart jug. Fill the 5-quart jug from the well twice, the first time dumping the water into one of the other containers.

(four inches)

280. Since both people used the same seven

letters, we can ignore the point values of all letters except C and E. It might seem at first glance that George's word was worth 4 points more—i.e., 3 points × 2 – 1 point × 2—but both people used both letters. George's points for the two letters were 3 × 2 + 1 = 7, while Lorna's points for these were 1 × 2 + 3 = 5, so George's word was worth 2 points more than Lorna's.

(5,280)

Pages 156–61

These grids work like crossword puzzle grids, except that digits, rather than letters, are written in the squares.

The first three problems are simply to give the students the experience of using the grid correctly. The other problems are fun to solve and teach the students that the logical place to start a solution is not necessarily at the first clue one encounters. They also teach that one may have to consider and discard various choices before finding one that satisfies all conditions.

ANSWERS

281. Four answers are possible because 1-A and 1-D can be exchanged, as can 4-D and 5-A.

1 4	2 2	▓
3 6	▓	4 2
▓	5 4	5

282. Two answers are possible because 1-A and 1-D can be exchanged.

1 2	2 7	▓
3 9	▓	4 1
▓	5 2	8

283. This is not possible. There are only four two-digit answers, and two of these (4-D and 5-A) must end with the same digit.

284. Emil's age, a two-digit number (1-D), is 3 more than Francine's age, a one-digit number (4-A), so his age is 11 or 12 (not 10, since 3-A can't be 0). But he is twice as old as Dorothy, so his age is an even number, 12. This forces 2-D, 4-A, and 5-A, and fills in all squares.

¹1	²6	▓
³2	▓	⁴9
▓	⁵2	4

285. Only three one-digit numbers—1, 2, and 3—have a one-digit square, and only one of these (3) has a two-digit cube. This forces 2-D, 4-A, and 1-D. 4-D, in the nineties, is divisible by 7 and so is 91 or 98, but only 91 works for 5-A.

¹2	²3	▓
³7	▓	⁴9
▓	⁵1	1

Pages 162–66

ANSWERS

286. 9514 + 948 = 10462

287. a. 1 1/2
b. 2/3
c. 3
d. 2 1/2
e. 4 1/2
f. 12
g. 5

288. a. $3.00
b. 50¢
c. 8
d. 6
e. Not enough information is given to answer this.

289. 1000

290. 1010101

291. 78

292. 12345678

293. 8, 16

294. 625

295. 1968 (Double the previous number.)

Page 167

When the students don't know the answer to a clue, they should be able to figure out for themselves that they can work in two directions—from the clues to the message and from the message to the clues. For example, if a word in the message is SE＿＿NTY and is known to be a number, the missing letters VE can be filled in there and then (from the numbers below those letters) can be transferred to the clue answers.

ANSWERS

296. a–g. The answers are as follows: product and subtract, eighty-nine, a fool, an abacus, twenty, AAA, whoops. The question and answer are, "What do you get if you chop down a banana tree? A banana split."

Page 168

The thing to realize about this problem is that each child works for six minutes to solve one problem.

ANSWERS

297. a. 6
b. 6
c. 24

Page 169

ANSWER

298. Put one ball in each pan. Either (1) the scale balances, or (2) the scale does not balance.

Suppose (1). Then the odd ball is one of the two unweighed. Remove one of the weighed balls and replace it with one of the two unweighed balls. If the scale balances, then the odd ball is the one still unweighed. If the scale doesn't balance, then the odd ball is the one that replaced the one removed. Suppose (2). Remove one ball from its pan and lay it aside. Replace the removed ball with one of the two unweighed balls. If the scale balances, then the odd ball is the one removed. If the scale doesn't balance, then the odd ball is the one not removed (the one left in the pan from the first weighing).

GLOSSARY

Words explained in the text are not listed here. To find the meaning of such a word, look in the Index for the page numbers where the word appears.

The definitions given here are as used in this book. See a dictionary for other definitions.

common factor—a factor that both of two numbers (or all of more than two numbers) have. (Examples: 2 is a common factor of 6, 10, and 18. 3 is not a common factor of 6, 10, and 18.)

digit (dij uht)—one part, or component, of a written number. (Example: 6, 3, and 7 are digits of 637.)

distinct (dis TING(K)T)—all different from each other. (Examples: 2, 3, and 4 are distinct. The numbers in the set {4,5,4} are not distinct.)

factor of a number—a divisor (of the number) that leaves no remainder. (Examples: 3 is a factor of 12; 8 is not a factor of 12.)

term—component or separate part. (Examples: Given the fraction $\frac{2}{3}$, its terms are 2 and 3; 2 is its first term, and 3 is its second term. Given a list of items, say

horse, bad-tempered old camel, baby elephant,

the list contains three terms, which are separated from each other by commas. The terms of a proportion are arranged like this:

$$\frac{\text{first term}}{\text{second term}} = \frac{\text{third term}}{\text{fourth term}})$$

INDEX

Alpha Centauri, 146. *Also see* Light-years.

Analogous. *Also see* Analogies, Analogy, reasoning by.

    reasoning, 85, 88, 89, 92, 97

    relationships, 29–36, 53, 56

Analogies, Analogy

    definition, 36

    in proportions, 104–22

    just for fun problems, 57–8

    rearranging, 55–8

    reasoning by, 36–9

    standard form, 53–6

Answers and Comments 173–96

Attributes

    finding common, 27

    identifying outsiders, 28

Balls. *See* Weighing balls.

Base. *Also see* Other bases.

    definition, 94

Celsius, 135–7

Clock arithmetic, 81–90

Counterexample, 44–52, 87, 88, 110

    definition, 44

Crossing a stream, 42

CrossNumber™ Puzzles, 16–20

Definitions. *See specific words.*

Diophantine problems, 43, 98, 125, 152

Directions. *See* Following directions.

Drawing inferences

    Hansel and Gretel, 9–12

    miscellaneous problems, 4–6, 13–5, 68–70

    Princess and the Frog, 7–8

Fahrenheit, 135–7

Fairy tales. *See* Drawing inferences.

Fantasy, 76–80

Following directions, 3, 148

Glossary, 197

Great-aunt Martha. *See* Math Mind Benders®.

Grid problems. *See* CrossNumber™ Puzzles, Math Mind Benders®, Mind Benders®, Puzzles.

Identifying opposites, 21

Identifying synonyms, 24

Index of refraction, 147. *Also see* Light-years.

Inferences. *See* Drawing inferences.

Letters, replacing with numbers, 162

Liars. *See* Truth-tellers and liars.

Light-year, 144–6

    definition, 144

Math Mind Benders®, 156–61

Measuring water. *See* Water jugs problems.

Messages. *See* Puzzles.

Middig, 51-2

Mind Benders®, 2, 74-5, 140–3, 149. *Also see* Math Mind Benders®.

Miscellaneous problems, 1, 101–2, 126, 155, 163–4, 168

    pig, 41

    postage rates, 150–1

    rainfall, snowfall, 163

Number patterns, 73, 165–6

Nursery rhymes. *See* Drawing inferences.

Odd balls. *See* Weighing balls.

Operations. *See* Operators.

Operators, 59–69

    definition, 59

    order of precedence, 59

Opposites, identifying, 21–3

Order of precedence. *See* Operators.

Other bases, 91–7

Patterns. See Number patterns.

Precedence, order of. *See* Operators.

Problems. *See specific category.*

Proof problems. *See* Proportions, proof problems.

Proportions, 104–22. *Also see* Ratios.

    analogies in, 104–6

    definition, 104

    extremes and means, 115

    hints for proof problems, 107

    means and extremes, 115

    proof problems, 108–22

    terms of, 107, 110, 111, 114, 115, 119–22

Proxima Centauri. *See* Alpha Centauri.

Puzzles. *Also see specific category.*

    numbered blanks, 167

    rearrange letters, 40, 99, 123, 139, 153

Ratios, 104, 108, 110, 114, 118, 120. *Also see* Proportions.

    definition, 104

Refraction. *See* Index of refraction.

Relevant

    definition, 127

    information, 127–34

Speed of light, 144, 147

Stream crossing. *See* Crossing a stream.

Synonyms, identifying, 24

Teaching Suggestions and Answers 171–96

Transitivity problems, 4–6, 70–2

Truth-tellers and liars, 75

Water jugs problems, 100, 124, 138, 154

Weighing balls, 103, 169

Zoffer, 51–2